OSPREY
PUBLISHING

Rorke's Drift 1879

'Pinned like rats in a hole'

Campaign • 41

OSPREY
PUBLISHING

Rorke's Drift 1879

'Pinned like rats in a hole'

Ian Knight • Illustrated by Michael & Alan Perry

Series editor Lee Johnson • Consultant editor David G Chandler

First published in Great Britain in 1996 by
Osprey Publishing, Elms Court, Chapel Way,
Botley, Oxford OX2 9LP,
United Kingdom.
Email: info@ospreypublishing.com

Reprinted 1996, 1997, 1998, 1999 (twice),
2001, 2002, 2003

ISBN 1 85532 506 3

CIP Data for this publication is
available from the British Library

Consultant Editor: DAVID G. CHANDLER
Series Editor: LEE JOHNSON
Designed by Paul Kime.

Colour bird's eye view illustrations by
Peter Harper.
Cartography by Micromap.
Battle scene artwork by Michael and
Alan Perry
Wargaming Rorke's Drift by Richard Brooks
& Ian Knight.

Filmset in Great Britain.
Printed in China through World Print Ltd.
FOR A CATALOGUE OF ALL BOOKS PUBLISHED BY
OSPREY MILITARY AND AVIATION PLEASE CONTACT:

The Marketing Manager, Osprey Direct UK,
PO Box 140, Wellingborough, Northants,
NN8 2FA, United Kingdom.
Email: info@ospreydirect.co.uk

The Marketing Manager, Osprey Direct USA,
c/o MBI Publishing, PO Box 1,
729 Prospect Avenue, Osceola, WI 54020, USA.
Email: info@ospreydirectusa.com

www.ospreypublishing.com

ACKNOWLEDGEMENTS

Many people over the years have encouraged my interest in the history of the Zulu, and given unselfishly of their own research. My greatest debt remains to S.B. Bourquin, who first took me camping at Rorke's Drift a decade ago, and my thanks are due too to Ian Castle, for his helpful advice during the planning stages of this book, to Keith Reeves and Rai England, who both allowed me access to their collections of illustrative material, and to Graeme Smythe, who made free with his hospitality at Rorke's Drift during several of my visits. Most of all my thanks are due to my wife Carolyn, who has shared my adventures in Zululand with patience and humour.

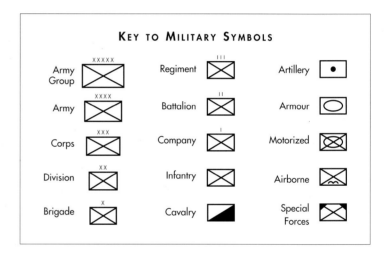

FRONT COVER Alphonse de Neuville's famous painting of the battle. (RRW Museum, Brecon)

CONTENTS

ORIGINS OF THE BATTLE

The battle of Rorke's Drift is not only the most famous engagement of the Anglo-Zulu War of 1879, but arguably one of the best known battles in the history of the British Army. The epic struggle against overwhelming odds, the undeniable valour of both sides, have invested it with a thrilling, *Boy's Own* Paper quality, which struck a chord with the British public at the time, and has inspired generations of authors and film-makers ever since. Yet in fact this particularly tough and brutal battle was fought to secure no very great strategic objective; it was little more than a mopping-up operation in the aftermath of a far more serious clash, and its true significance was largely a moral one – it rescued British prestige on a day when the army of the greatest imperial power in the world had been dramatically and unexpectedly humbled.

European involvement in southern Africa dated back to the beginning of the 17th century, when the Dutch had established a small toe-hold on the Cape of Good Hope, to service their ships on the long haul to the

LEFT *The Hero of Rorke's Drift; a splendid formal portrait of John Chard, taken shortly after the Zulu War. He is wearing his Victoria Cross and South African campaign medal, and his full dress uniform is in stark contrast to the more practical undress he seems to have worn during the battle. (Royal Engineers' Museum)*

RIGHT *The Swedish mission station at Rorke's Drift, sketched before the outbreak of hostilities. The post commanded one of the principal gateways into the Zulu kingdom. (Author's photo)*

Indies, the focus of intense rivalry among the burgeoning imperial powers of Europe. With the coming of the Revolutionary and Napoleonic wars, the European powers found themselves at war around the globe, and ownership of the Cape changed several times, finally coming to rest in the hands of the British. There was little to attract colonial interest in the Cape beyond its strategic significance, and neither the Dutch nor the British had been inclined to expand their territory there.

The first Dutch settlers had developed into a hardy and independent breed, however, who constantly wandered beyond the enclave's official boundaries in search of good grazing land, pushing out the bounds of European influence and dragging authority reluctantly in their wake. This process was underway before the arrival of the British, but the instinctive dislike which the Dutch *boere* soon conceived for their new masters intensified it. By the 1830s many Boers were openly trekking away from British rule in an attempt to establish their own lands, free of outside interference, in the interior. Of course, almost all of southern Africa was already claimed by one indigenous group or other, and the progress of these Boer Voortrekkers was marked by a series of sharp and bloody conflicts with robust African societies. Against her better judgement, Britain found herself cast in the role of imperial policeman; ironically, by trying to break away from the British, the Boers merely provoked them into extending their authority still further.

The mission station in 1881, after the Reverend Witt had rebuilt his house, which was burnt down in the battle. The new house stands on the spot previously occupied by the old hospital; this new building greatly resembles the original. (S.B. Bourquin)

By the middle of the 19th century a stalemate of sorts had been reached. Britain controlled two colonies, the Cape and Natal, which stretched more or less from the tip of the continent around the eastern sea-board, almost as far as Portuguese Mozambique, while the Boers held two independent republics in the interior, the Orange Free State and the Transvaal. Sandwiched in between, hard-pressed both militarily and economically, were what remained of the original African groups. The strongest of these was the Zulu kingdom, which lay to the north of Natal, across the Thukela and Mzinyathi rivers. The Zulu kingdom had emerged in the 1820s from a period of fierce internecine struggle, and had once laid claim to much of Natal itself; in 1824, however, the Zulu king Shaka kaSenzangakhona had

Sir Henry Bartle Frere (centre) and his staff. Frere saw the powerful and independent Zulu kingdom as a potential threat to the policy of Confederation, and set about engineering a confrontation with the Zulus. (Natal Archives)

granted trading rights to a handful of largely British adventurers who had established themselves at Port Natal (later Durban) This concession was the basis of all subsequent British claims to the area, and from this point on the fortunes of the Zulu kingdom were inextricably entwined with British Colonial policy in the region. Despite the odd scare, relations between the Zulu kingdom and British Natal remained largely friendly for almost 50 years. Gradually, however, the presence within Zululand of a strong central government, which resisted Colonial influence and was manifest in a sophisticated military system, came to be seen by the British as problematic. In the 1870s Britain adopted a new forward policy in southern Africa, stimulated by the discovery of diamonds at Kimberley, which offered the potential for hitherto unsuspected economic development. The object of this policy – called 'Confederation' – was to bring all of the disparate groups under British control, so that a new political and economic infrastructure could be imposed across the region as a whole. In 1877 Britain annexed the Transvaal, and with it inherited a long-standing border dispute between that republic and the Zulu kingdom. Very soon the British high commissioner, Sir Henry Bartle Frere, came to see the existence of the

Zulu kingdom as a threat to the Confederation policy, and deliberately set about provoking a military confrontation to break its power.

Neither Frere nor his commander in the field, Lieutenant-General Lord Chelmsford, expected the Zulu campaign to be either long or difficult. By a careful count, they estimated that the Zulu king, Cetshwayo kaMpande, could field upwards of 40,000 warriors, but while these were well disciplined and well trained, they were essentially a part-time citizen army, and were armed primarily with traditional weapons. They were thought to be no match for a modern professional army. Indeed, shortly before the outbreak of the Anglo-Zulu War, Chelmsford had brought to a successful conclusion a messy campaign against the Xhosa people on the Eastern Cape frontier. Then he had managed a mixed force of regular troops, Colonial volunteers and African auxiliaries, under difficult circumstances, operating in broken and heavily wooded terrain against a foe who preferred hit-and-run tactics to an open fight. Although the home government was reluctant to approve Frere's overtly confrontational approach, and refused to send Chelmsford more than a handful of reinforcements, Chelmsford remained convinced that he could win a Zulu war with the tried and experienced troops already under his command. Whatever his own advisors might say of the fighting potential of the Zulu, Chelmsford could not quite bring himself to believe that they were, at heart, any different from the Xhosa whom he had already faced. He entered the Anglo-Zulu War convinced that the Zulu would not stand against him, and would need to be driven into a corner and made to fight; this was a misconception that, in due course, would be quite comprehensively disabused.

In December 1878 Frere's representatives presented King Cetshwayo with a series of demands which they knew he could not accept. They allowed him 30 days to consider them, and in the meantime Chelmsford began to assemble his forces on the Zulu borders. He planned initially to invade Zululand in five separate columns, converging on the Zulu king's main residence at oNdini (Ulundi). He hoped thereby to pin the Zulu army down and bring it to battle, while at the same time allowing it no room to slip past him and make a counter-strike into Colonial Natal. In fact, lack of troops and the tremendous problems of keeping so many columns supplied in the field forced him to reduce the number of striking columns to three and keep the other two in reserve. The British troops had reached their assembly point by the first week of January 1879, and when the Zulu king failed to respond to the terms of the ultimatum, Chelmsford's troops crossed the border on 11 January, and the Anglo-Zulu War began.

OPPOSING PLANS

Lord Chelmsford himself opted to accompany the Central Column, which was both the strongest and the best placed to strike directly into the Zulu heartland. It consisted of two battalions of regular infantry – the 1st and 2nd Bn., 24th Regiment (2nd Warwickshires), a battery of 7-pdr. field guns, a regiment of the locally-raised Natal Native Contingent (NNC) and a small cavalry force composed of local volunteers and mounted infantry. He fully expected that the Central Column would bear the brunt of the fighting, with the two flanking columns acting in support, and so, indeed, it proved.

The column had assembled in December 1878 at Helpmekaar, on a high, windy ridge that overlooked the Mzinyathi river, which marked the central stretch of the Zulu border. Helpmekaar consisted of nothing more than a couple of buildings, but it was chosen because of its strategic location. It

BELOW *Fort Bromhead in late 1879. A small portion of the hospital wall has been left standing and incorporated into the wall of the new fort (left). The British cemetery is in the foreground; it was across this ground that the initial Zulu attack took place. (S.B. Bourquin)*

lay astride a wagon track which stretched back through the spectacular Thukela valley to the Colonial capital, Pietermaritzburg, and from there all the way to Durban. It offered Chelmsford a secure and viable line of communication and supply, and beyond Helpmekaar an old trader's wagon-track dropped down to cross the Mzinyathi at Rorke's Drift. Roads into Zululand were scarce enough, and over the years Rorke's Drift had become one of the main gateways into the kingdom. It was named after an Irish hunter and trader, Jim Rorke, who had bought a farm in the region in the 1840s, not long after Natal had been proclaimed a British colony. Rorke had lived an adventurous life, hunting the last of the elephant in the

A British camp at Rorke's Drift, with the Mzinyathi (Buffalo) and the Drift itself in the background. This photograph was probably taken in June 1879, but the scene would not have been markedly different when the invasion began in January. (S.B. Bourquin)

Mzinyathi valley, and had traded across the river with the Zulus. He had built a house and a store in the shade of a hill which overlooked the drift; the Zulus knew the hill as Shiyane, 'the eyebrow', and Rorke's post as KwaJim – Jim's place. Rorke had died in the 1870s, and his widow had sold the farm to a Swedish mission society, who had installed a Reverend Otto Witt as incumbent. Witt had renamed the hill Oskarsberg, after the King of Sweden, and used Rorke's store as a church, but beyond that had made few changes by the time war broke out.

For Chelmsford, Rorke's Drift offered as good a route into Zululand as any that was available. The countryside upstream was comparatively open, affording a view of several miles of enemy territory, but a few miles below Shiyane the hills closed in on either side of the Mzinyathi, forcing the river into a series of gorges which marked the line of the border almost as far as the sea. The drift itself was a secure one, since a shelf of sandstone ensured that the river was fordable except in time of severest flood. Rorke's buildings were perhaps half a mile from the river, with sufficient view of it to make the position a commanding one. Furthermore, Chelmsford would need to ferry his supplies to the front by stages, and the buildings allowed him to establish a supply depot on the border itself.

When Chelmsford moved down from Helpmekaar in the first week of January, he took over Witt's buildings, using one as a makeshift hospital and packing the other with sacks and crates of supplies. Witt's attitude to this intrusion is not clear; he was a humanitarian man, but like many in the missionary community, he may have welcomed confrontation with King Cetshwayo's administration, which was known to be opposed to Christian evangelism in Zululand.

The crossing at Rorke's Drift from the Zulu bank; on the day of the invasion, the 2nd Battalion, 24th Regiment lined the rise opposite, while the 1st Bn. crossed on the ponts (left). The mission station is just visible on the skyline (left). This photo was taken c. June 1879, when a secure redoubt – Fort Melvill – had been built to command the crossing. (Killie Campbell Library)

RORKE'S DRIFT, 11 JANUARY, THE INVASION BEGINS

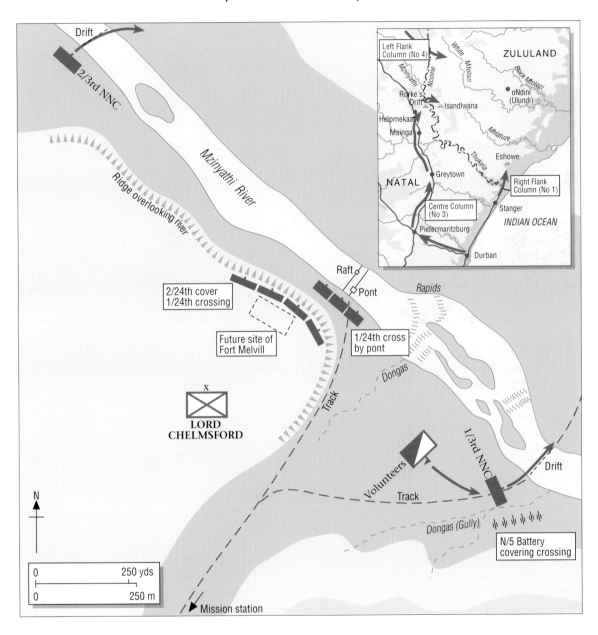

Much of Natal had been afflicted by drought throughout the 1870s, but in late 1878 the weather had broken, and when the ultimatum expired, Chelmsford was faced with moving into hostile territory across a flooded Mzinyathi. To help with the crossing, hawsers were fixed across the river so that a portable flat-bottomed ferry, known as a pont, could be operated, together with an improvised barrel-raft. Both ferries could hold either a transport wagon and its oxen or a full company of infantry at a time.

The crossing took place on the damp and murky morning of 11 January. The black auxiliaries of the NNC were ordered to cross on foot above and below the pont, where the water was chest-deep, while the regular infantry were ferried across in between. It was an anxious moment, since Chelmsford was worried that the mist might conceal a Zulu impi (armed force) lying in wait on the other bank; the artillery were unlimbered on the Natal side, ready to provide covering fire. Yet when the sun finally rose and the mist burned off, there were no Zulus in sight, and the crossing proceeded without incident. Chelmsford's troops built their first camp in enemy territory on the Zulu bank overlooking the Drift.

Immediately across Chelmsford's line of advance lay the Batshe stream, the home of the Zulu chief Sihayo kaXongo. Sihayo's followers had been involved in a border transgression six months before, and Chelmsford was eager both to make some demonstration of force against them and to test the mettle of the enemy. Before dawn on 12 January, therefore, just a day after the war had begun, he took part of his force and struck at Sihayo's homesteads. Most Zulu men had abandoned their homes to join the main army mustering at oNdini, but some of Sihayo's retainers had stayed to protect his property. As the British advanced, the Zulus took up a secure position among the boulders at the foot of a line of cliffs overlooking the Batshe valley. Chelmsford executed the attack according to the tactics he had successfully employed on the Cape frontier, sending parties up the hills on either side and using his auxiliaries to make a frontal assault. The

The pont at Rorke's Drift, with Shiyane hill behind; on 22 January Lieutenant Chard RE was supervising repairs of these ferries when news of the disaster reached him. This photo was taken some months after the battle. (Killie Campbell Library)

16

The Centre Column crossing at Rorke's Drift, 11 January 1879. Note the ponts, centre, and the Native Contingent crossing right. The crag of Isandlwana is on the skyline.

Zulus were heavily outnumbered, but there was a sharp fight before they were evicted. The incident reinforced Chelmsford's view that the fighting capabilities of the Zulu had been overrated, and that the open-order tactics he had become accustomed to were, indeed, the correct ones.

ISANDLWANA

Chelmsford did not intend to remain on the border, and once the main column had crossed the river, the post at Rorke's Drift was effectively relegated to the role of a depot on the line of communication. Stores were constantly brought down from Helpmekaar, stockpiled out of the rain in the buildings, then ferried forward across the river; there were a handful of Commissariat officers to supervise them, but the dull and routine work of garrisoning the post fell to one company of the 24th Regiment and a company of the NNC. Had events turned out otherwise, it might have proved a safe way for them to sit out the war.

Chelmsford's advance did not proceed as rapidly as he might have hoped. The same rains that had swollen the Mzinyathi – and which descended in a deluge on his troops almost nightly – had turned the track into a quagmire. The passage of even a few heavily laden transport wagons was enough to break it up completely. Chelmsford established a temporary camp near Sihayo's stronghold, and for more than a week his engineers struggled to make the road serviceable. It was not until 20 January that he felt able to make the next stage of his advance, and he chose as his base the forward slope at the foot of a distinctive rocky outcrop known as Isandlwana.

It is worth noting that at this stage, no attempt had been made to fortify any of the British camps, either at Rorke's Drift or in Zululand. Chelmsford's standing orders suggested that camps should be secured, but the precaution had seldom been necessary on the Cape frontier, and the absence of any serious Zulu opposition so far had encouraged a complacency which stretched from the general himself down. When Chelmsford arrived at Isandlwana on the 20th, he did not expect to stay there long; almost immediately patrols were sent out looking for the next viable camping-ground. This was despite clear indications that there was a Zulu presence in the vicinity: Chelmsford's spies suggested that the main Zulu army had left oNdini a few days before, and was likely to advance against the Centre Column which, after the skirmish at Sihayo's, was perceived by the Zulus as being the most dangerous. Even by the time he reached Isandlwana, Chelmsford was anticipating a confrontation, but the prospect did not worry him; indeed, his greatest fear was that the Zulus would refuse to give battle directly, but try to slip around his flank and strike into Natal. The track towards oNdini was bordered by a range of hills which extended towards his right until they reached the Mzinyathi. Any force coming from the Zulu capital might slip into these hills, and accord-

THE ISANDLWANA CAMPAIGN, OPERATIONS 11-22 JANUARY 1879

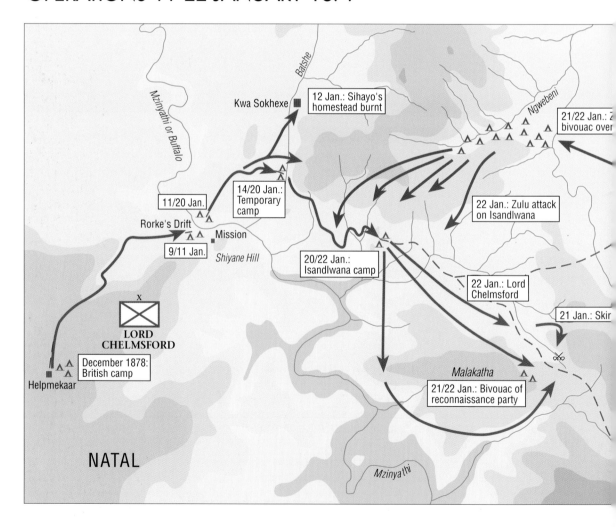

ingly Chelmsford sent a strong probe into them on 21 January. That night, part of this probe ran into a body of warriors, who fell back before them, skilfully using the terrain and dusk to prevent the British getting a good impression of their strength.

When the news was reported to Lord Chelmsford, it exactly confirmed his expectations. Here was a Zulu force where he expected to find it, and avoiding battle under cover of darkness. Afraid that the Zulus might slip away, Chelmsford therefore ordered roughly half his force to march out from Isandlwana before dawn the next day to confront them. He left approximately 1,700 British troops and their African allies to guard the camp at Isandlwana. Chelmsford was acting logically, according to the best information at his disposal, and yet, almost certainly by accident, the Zulus

Hand-to-hand fighting beneath the distinctive crag of Isandlwana; Lord Chelmsford's defeat on 22 January threw the British invasion plans into confusion, and left the way open for the Zulu attack on Rorke's Drift. (Author's collection)

19

led him to commit a fatal mistake. The warriors encountered on the previous night were not the main army, but merely stragglers moving in its wake. In fact the main army had already moved across Chelmsford's front, masking its advance with a line of hills, and lay close to the camp's left flank. While Chelmsford spent the morning of 22 January 12 miles away, fruitlessly searching for the enemy, scouts from the British camp blundered into the Zulu army, concealed in a valley just five miles from Isandlwana. The Zulus had not intended to attack that morning, but the encounter provoked them, and they rose up and advanced rapidly on the camp.

Almost all the British officers holding commands at Isandlwana failed to appreciate the danger until it was too late; they deployed their men in open order some distance from the camp, believing that they were facing no more than a local force. It was not until the Zulu army came fully into view, some 20,000 of them cresting the entire line of a range of hills overlooking the camp, that the British realised how badly they had underestimated their foe.

The Zulus advanced in their traditional attack formation (the 'horns of the bull'), a dense body (the 'chest') moving straight at the camp, while encircling parties ('the horns') were flung out on either side. For a while the steady fire of the regular infantry kept the Zulu centre at bay, but the line was over-extended and in danger of being outflanked. Too late the British realised the danger and tried to fall back and regroup, but the Zulus rushed in and pierced the line. The British formations were broken up and driven back through the camp until cut off by the encircling horns. Only a trickle or survivors slipped through and escaped; for most of those within the cordon there was no option but to fight to the death. Some 1,300 of the garrison were killed, including all the infantry out in the firing line; most of the survivors were black auxiliaries, and fewer than 60 white troops managed to escape the slaughter.

THE APPROACH TO RORKE'S DRIFT

The battle of Isandlwana had taken place, curiously, almost without planning on either side. Although both the British and the Zulu had expected an imminent confrontation, the actual encounter had taken both by surprise, and the battle had developed spontaneously. It was the Zulus who recovered first, enabling them to maintain the initiative, forcing the defending garrison to react to their attack until eventually they were overstretched. Lord Chelmsford and the men under his command – the one group who had expected to fight that day – took no part in the action, and remained unaware of it until it was over. This lack of preparation was even more apparent during the attack on Rorke's Drift, which resulted entirely from the Zulu momentum at Isandlwana.

It was usual for a Zulu army to form into a circle immediately before battle, to hear the commanders' instructions, and to undergo last minute pre-combat rituals. When British scouts had unexpectedly discovered the impi just before noon, however, there had been no time for such niceties; the nearest regiments had simply risen and advanced, drawing the rest of the army after them. The senior commanders were only able to restrain the regiments furthest from the encounter, who had arrived late at the bivouac and were therefore on the end of the line. There were four of them, the uThulwana, iNdlondlo, uDloko and iNdluyengwe, with a combined strength of over 6,000 men. They were directed to form the reserve, and to advance behind the attacking regiments in the wake of the right horn, so as to move round behind Isandlwana and cut the road to Rorke's Drift, and with it the British line of retreat.

The movement of the Zulu right was so successful that when the British were driven back through the camp, they found to their horror that the road was already cut, and that the right horn was deploying to attack them from behind Isandlwana. A handful of fugitives were spewed out by the fighting and fled pell-mell across country, harried by those warriors who were not exhausted by the attack on the camp. Unable to reach Rorke's Drift, the survivors struck the Mzinyathi a few miles downstream, where a narrow gorge concealed a dubious crossing known as Sothondose's Drift. Because the river was high, the drift was submerged beneath a roaring torrent of water, and many fugitives reached the border only to be swept away in the river and drowned. For the most part the Zulu reserve kept clear of the fighting behind Isandlwana, moving at an even pace across country to strike the river mid-way between Rorke's Drift and Sothondose's Drift. To stem the flow of survivors, however, the iNdluyengwe were despatched to catch the fugitives on the heights above Sothondose's Drift, driving them down the rocky slopes and slaughtering them right down to the banks of the river itself.

The river presented a formidable barrier to the Zulus too, and not just a physical one. When the great army had mustered at oNdini less than a week before, King Cetshwayo had instructed it not to cross into Natal territory. He felt himself to be the victim of unwarranted British aggression, and he wanted to emphasise the point by waging a strictly defensive campaign. This, he hoped, would stand him in good stead during any subsequent peace negotiations. In the heat of battle, many warriors had chased the British survivors all the way from the camp at Isandlwana to the river, scouring the bush to flush out any who might be hiding, but they were, by that time, beginning to suffer the effects of fatigue, and most were quite happy to recall the king's orders and abandon the pursuit rather than cross the border. A few of the more adventurous had prepared to cross the river, but some of the king's *izinduna* (officers) had called them back. There were, in any case, many wounded to attend to, and their great prize, the British camp, was ripe for looting. By mid-afternoon on 22 January the Zulu attack was largely spent, and the warriors were preparing to retire the way they had come, carrying off with them the fruits of their victory, both sweet and sour – all the exotic delights of the British camp and hundreds of their own wounded men. For the reserve, however, the battle was not over. Apart from the iNdluyengwe, the reserve regiments had played almost no part in the action. They were senior men – veterans – who could expect a hard time from their wives and families if they returned home with no stories to tell of heroic deeds and no booty. Although the British were later convinced that the Zulu had been intent on invading Natal, this was not the case; the reserve was already tired by the time it crossed the border, and would have been in no condition to undertake prolonged campaigning. Nor were they in sufficient strength to take on the British garrisons scattered throughout Natal. Their aims were much more limited: questioned after the war, their commander, Prince Dabulamanzi kaMpande, admitted that he had been motivated by no greater desire than to 'wash the spears of his boys' in the blood of the British. It was probably common knowledge among the Zulus that the British had established a post at KwaJim's, and in the aftermath of the great victory at Isandlwana it must have seemed a very small thing to indulge in a minor raid across the border, mopping up the surviving garrisons there and seizing their stockpile of supplies. (Presumably Prince Dabulamanzi relied on his close blood-relationship with the king – they

THE APPROACH TO RORKE'S DRIFT, 22 JANUARY 1879, 1300-1630

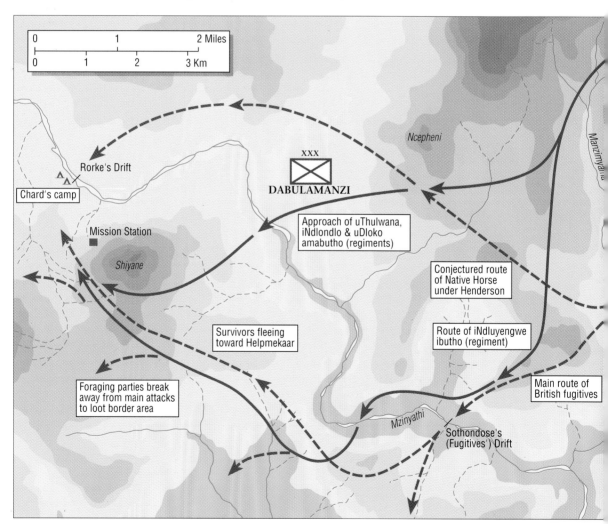

were half-brothers — to protect him from the repercussions of disobeying a royal command.) The iNdluyengwe crossed the river at a narrow gorge just above Fugitives' Drift, while the remaining regiments moved a few miles upstream, to where the river was wider and shallower.

AT RORKE'S DRIFT

Since the main column's move forward to Isandlwana, life had been quiet at Rorke's Drift. A party of six Royal Engineers of No. 5 Company, under Lieutenant John Chard, had arrived from Durban on 19 January, and had pitched their tents on a rise overlooking the crossing. The ponts were showing signs of wear from the constant traffic across the river, and it was Chard's duty to keep them in working order. Upwards of 30 wagon-loads of supplies had been hauled down from Helpmekaar to supply the new camp, and were waiting to go forward across the river; a convoy was expected to collect them on 22 January. The storehouse was packed from floor to ceiling with bags of mealies, weighing 200lbs each, and heavy crates of army biscuit, and still there was enough left over to form two huge piles in front of the storehouse veranda. The supplies were under the command of a handful of Commissariat officers led by Assistant Commissary Walter Dunne, but the overall command of the post fell to Major Spalding, Deputy Acting Adjutant and Quartermaster-General, who was in charge of that stretch of the line of communication. The Reverend Witt had not yet abandoned his post, but had made rooms in his house available to about 30 sick men in the care of Surgeon James Reynolds of the Army Medical Department. Although one or two of these men had been wounded in the fighting during the attack on at Sihayo's homestead, most were suffering from a typical range of illnesses or injuries which afflicted men on campaign in Africa — diarrhoea, dysentery, broken limbs and sprains. The post was guarded by one company of the 2nd/24th, B Company, under Lieutenant Gonville Bromhead, and a company of the 2nd/3rd NNC, under Captain Stevenson.

On the morning of 22 January Chard received unambiguous orders from the staff at Isandlwana, ordering his men forward to the camp. Unsure whether the order included himself, he rode forward with them to find out, but was told he was required to remain at the Drift to build an entrenchment to protect the crossing. Before he set off on the return journey, however, he heard the first reports of Zulu movements near the camp. Leaving his men at Isandlwana — to be killed with the rest, as he later regretted — Chard rode back to Rorke's Drift and expressed his concern to Major Spalding that the Zulus might try to slip round behind the column and strike at the Drift. No defensive arrangements had yet been made to protect the post, and a company of the 24th due down from Helpmekaar to reinforce it was several days overdue. Spalding decided to ride back to Helpmekaar to chivvy them along; before he left he flicked through a copy of the Army List, and rode off remarking casually: 'I see you are senior, so you will be in charge, although of course nothing will happen, and I shall be back again this evening early.' Chard seems to have been reassured by this, and retired to his tent to enjoy lunch and write letters home.

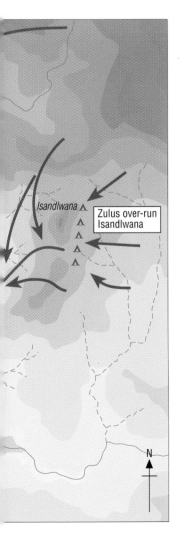

Isandlwana

Zulus over-run Isandlwana

N

Surgeon James Henry Reynolds, in charge of the hospital at Rorke's Drift at the time of the battle. (Royal Archives)

The first distant shots from Isandlwana could be heard at Rorke's Drift shortly after noon. They provoked curiosity among the garrison rather than alarm; it was assumed that Lord Chelmsford was defeating the Zulus, and the garrison were, if anything, disappointed at missing the action. Three men whose duties were not particularly pressing – Surgeon Reynolds, Otto Witt and a local padre, George Smith, who was acting as unofficial chaplain to the Column – decided to climb the Shiyane hill, to see if they could see anything of the battle. It was a hot day, and the climb probably took them half an hour; from the top, through a spy-glass, they could see something of the fighting around Isandlwana, although the mountain itself blocked out the view of the momentous events in front of the camp. They noted several lines of black troops working across country towards the Mzinyathi, led by two officers on horseback, but simply took them to be men of the NNC returning to the Drift. It was only when they drew close enough for the observers to spot that the officers too were black that they experienced the first sense of unease. Scrambling down the hill rather quicker than they had gone up, they returned to the post to raise the alarm.

In fact news of the disaster had already reached the men at the post and Chard at the river. Sometime after 3.00pm Chard saw two men ride up to the far bank and hail him; when he sent the pont across to fetch them, they proved to be Lieutenant Adendorff of the NNC and a Carbineer. Adendorff took Chard to one side and told him the news; it was so shock-

Gonville Bromhead, the commander of B Company, promoted to major and wearing his VC. (Royal Archives)

ing that for a few minutes Chard couldn't take it in, and went so far as to suggest that Adendorff had not stayed long enough to witness the outcome of the battle. Yet something was clearly wrong, and when Chard and Adendorff rode up to the post to consult with the officers there, they found that the news had already been broken by a stream of exhausted and terrified survivors who had ridden past from the direction of Sothondose's Drift. Most of these men were utterly spent, and rode on in the direction of Helpmekaar.

Yet the news of Isandlwana was garbled, and, if anything, Chard probably understood that the situation was even worse than it actually was; Chelmsford's column had been destroyed, and the Zulus were making their way across country to Rorke's Drift. The enemy's strength was unknown, but the information from the observers on the hill suggested that they would arrive within the hour. Should the garrison stay and fight, or try to fall back on Helpmekaar? Lieutenant Bromhead had already made preparations for both eventualities. There were two wagons at the post, and these he ordered up close to the buildings, ready to evacuate the patients if necessary. Should they decide to stay, however, he had ordered the men to drag out the mealie-bags and biscuit-boxes from the store, ready to form barricades. While Chard and Bromhead were discussing their options, a Commissariat officer, Acting Assistant James Langley Dalton, apparently spoke up in favour of making a stand. Dalton was a former sergeant of the 85th Regiment, an imposing man whose experience and manner gave him an authority which belied his rank. He pointed out that if the garrison abandoned the post and fell back on Helpmekaar, encumbered as they were by wagons carrying the sick, the Zulus would be sure to overtake them on the road. Caught in the open and heavily outnumbered, they stood no chance; at least Jim Rorke's buildings offered them a secure bastion around which to make a defence. Chard and Bromhead agreed: the garrison would make a stand.

OPPOSING ARMIES

THE BRITISH GARRISON

The troops who had so suddenly and unexpectedly found themselves in the frontline were a representative cross-section of the British army in Zululand. At full strength an infantry company consisted of 100 men, though it was seldom up to scratch due to sickness and detached duties. However, B Company had 95 men available for duty that day.

The 2nd/24th had only been in Africa since March 1878, arriving in time to take part in the last skirmishes of the Cape Frontier War, and their composition therefore reflected a number of changes which had taken place in army organisation at home. Although officially titled the 2nd Warwickshires, the 24th's depot had been established at Brecon, in south Wales, in 1873. From then on there was a marked increase in the number of men recruited along the Anglo-Welsh borders. This had had only a limited effect on the 1st Battalion, because it had been stationed overseas since that time, and had received only a few drafts from the depot before Isandlwana. There was undoubtedly a high proportion of Welshmen in the 2nd Battalion, but, like any unit in the Victorian army, it included a significant number of English, Irish and Scotsmen. Not least among the many myths about Rorke's Drift is that it was defended entirely by Welshmen.

The introduction of the short-service system as part of the Cardwell reforms had meant that recruits had to spend only six years with the Colours and six in reserve, rather than all 12 with the Colours, and this had the effect of attracting a better class of man and bringing down the age of the average soldier. This was evident in the composition of the 2nd Battalion, many of whom were young men in their mid-twenties. The senior NCO of B Company, Colour-Sergeant Frank Bourne, was just 24 at the time of the battle, and known to his men as 'The Kid'. Nevertheless, B Company was not without experience, for it had learned something of the realities of campaigning in the harsh South African climate and terrain on the Cape Frontier, and the men had faced the 'whiz and rip' of Xhosa spears, and learned to stand by one another and to trust their officer, Lieutenant Bromhead.

B Company were armed with a single-shot breech-loading rifle, the Martini-Henry, which threw a heavy .450 calibre unjacketed lead slug to a maximum range of over 1,000 yards, but was most effective at less than

Lieutenant-Colonel Frank Bourne, photographed in later life. Bourne was just 24 at the time of the battle, B Company's colour-sergeant, and is thought to have been the longest surviving veteran of the battle; he died in 1945. (RRW Museum, Brecon)

The defenders of Rorke's Drift; B Company, 2nd/24th. This photograph was taken at the end of the Anglo-Zulu War, when many of those injured in the battle had been invalided home. Some of those who distinguished themselves in the action are therefore not present. Lt. Bromhead is sitting on the left of the front row, however, looking off, while Colour-sergeant Bourne is on the extreme left of the second row. (S.B. Bourquin)

400 yards. For the ORs it was topped by an 18-in. socket bayonet whose wicked reach had earned it the nick-name 'the lunger', while sergeants carried a heavy sword bayonet. The men's uniforms, scarlet jackets with green regimental facings, blue trousers and white sun-helmets, were perhaps more suited to the parade ground than the battlefield, but B Company had already learned the veteran's trick of dulling the helmet and pouches with dyes made from tea or coffee, and several months of hard campaigning would have left the tunics faded, patched and ragged.

Estimates of the number of black troops at Rorke's Drift vary between 100 and 300. Ordinarily a company of the Natal Native Contingent should have consisted of three white officers, six white NCOs, one black officer, ten black NCOs and 90 black privates, but it seems that more men had rather arbitrarily been left with the company on the border. The NNC had been raised among the black population of Natal, many of whom were closely linked with the Zulus but had a tradition of hostility to the Zulu royal house. Their potential was considerable, but they had only been raised in late 1878, just a month or two before the war started; there had been little time to train them, and few good officers to appoint to their command. Furthermore, because the Natal authorities had been concerned lest they pose a threat to internal security, the decision had been taken to arm only one in ten of them with firearms. Even these had scarcely any training in their use. The rest fought with their own shields and spears. Although a few officers had made attempts to procure old military tunics for their men, most were distinguished by nothing more than a red rag twisted around their heads.

The 30 sick, under the care of Surgeon Reynolds and three men of the Army Hospital Corps, were likely to be acutely vulnerable in the coming fight, although in fact only a handful were so incapacitated that they could not defend themselves. Some of the more able patients left the hospital building to man the ramparts elsewhere, while the rest were given rifles

and told to defend their rooms. The Commissariat officers – Assistant Commissary Dunne, Acting Assistant Commissary Dalton and civilian store-keeper Mr Byrne – supervised the distribution of the mealie bags and biscuit boxes to make barricades.

With 400 men to build them, the barricades went up fast. Rorke's post consisted of two long thatched bungalows, 30 yards apart, built about 300 yards from a line of broken strata which marked the base of Shiyane hill. The storehouse – Witt's church – was the bigger of the two, about 80 ft by 20 ft, while the hospital – Witt's house – was 60 ft by 18 ft. Both build-ings had open verandas at the front. A wooden staircase ran up the outside wall at the western end of the storehouse, to an attic under the eaves, and there were several supporting buttresses at the back. The store was rela-tively secure, since there were no doors or windows along the back wall, but the hospital was more problematic. Rorke seems not to have had a very clear sense of interior design, for the building was a warren of small rooms with no interconnecting corridor, and several rooms did not open into each other, but directly to the outside. Both the back and the side walls included a number of doors and windows. The general feeling among the garrison was that the loss of either building would spell the end of the post, so it was decided to leave the patients where they were, and to place half a dozen able-bodied men in the hospital to assist in its defence. Taking a pick-axe with them, these men knocked holes through the outside walls to serve as loopholes, and blocked up the doors and windows with mealie-bags and biscuit-boxes. As Chard admitted later, however, it occurred to no one at this stage to knock a passage through the internal walls to make movement between the rooms easier.

Rorke had built his buildings on a flat shelf which dropped away a few feet in front of them in a bank four or five feet high. In front of the hos-pital this drop was little more than a steep slope, but in places between the buildings it was a broken ledge shoulder-high. The storehouse was set back slightly, and a well-built stone cattle-kraal lay on its right front corner.

B Company, 2nd/24th, probably photographed at Pinetown, Natal, shortly before leaving South Africa at the end of the Anglo-Zulu War. Lt. Bromhead is the blurred figure on the left; Colour-sergeant Bourne stands next to him. (Local History Museum, Durban)

Fragments of sacking found at Rorke's Drift during an archaeological survey, and believed to be remains from the original mealie-bag barricade. (Author's photo)

ORDER OF BATTLE, RORKE'S DRIFT, 22-23 JANUARY 1879

THE ZULUS

Commander
Prince Dabulamanzi kaMpande

iNdluyengwe ibutho 500–700 men (approx.)

uThulwana
iNdlondlo } 3000 men total
uDloko } (approx)

THE BRITISH

Officer Commanding
Lieutenant J.R.M. Chard, 5th (Field) Company, Royal Engineers

Staff
Sergeant G.W. Mabin.

Royal Artillery
Bombadier T. Lewis
Wheeler J. Cantwell
Gunners A. Evans and A. Howard

5th Field Company, Royal Engineers
Driver E. Robson

2nd Battalion, 3rd (East Kent) Regiment (The Buffs)
Sergeant F. Millne

1st Battalion, 24th Regiment
Sergeant E. Wilson
Privates W. Beckett, P. Desmond, W. Horrigan, J. Jenkins, E. Nicholas, T. Payton, W. Roy, H. Turner, J. Waters

2nd Battalion, 24th Regiment
Lieutenant G. Bromhead
Colour-Sergeant F. Bourne

Sergeants
H. Gallagher, R. Maxfield, G. Smith, J. Windridge.

Lance-Sergeants
J. Taylor, T. Williams

Corporals
W. Allen, G. French, J. Key, J. Lyons (1112), A. Saxty.

Lance-Corporals
W. Bessell, W. Halley

Drummers
P. Galgey, P. Hayes, J. Keefe, J. Meehan.

Privates
R. Adams, J. Ashton, T. Barry, W. Bennett, J. Bly, J. Bromwich, T. Buckley, T. Burke, J. Bushe, W.H. Camp, T. Chester, J. Chick, T. Clayton, R. Cole, T. Cole, T. Collins, J. Connolly, A. Conners, T. Conners, W. Cooper, G. Davis, W.H. Davis, T. Daw, G. Deacon, M. Deane, J. Dick, W. Dicks, T. Driscoll, J. Dunbar, G. Edwards, J. Fagan, E. Gee, J. Hagan, J. Harris, G. Haydon, F. Hitch, A.H. Hook, J. Jobbins, E. Jones, J. Jones (970), J. Jones (1179), R. Jones, W. Jones, P. Judge, P. Kears, M. Kiley, D. Lewis, H. Lines, D. Lloyd, T. Lockhart, J. Lodge, T.M. Lynch, J. Lyons (1441), J. Manley, J. Marshall, H. Martin, C. Mason, M. Minehan, T. Moffatt, A. Morris, F. Morris, T. Morrison, J. Murphy, W. Neville, R. Norris, W. Osbourne, S. Parry, W. Partridge, S. Pitts, T. Robinson, J. Ruck, E. Savage, J. Scanlon, A. Sears, G. Shearman, J. Shergold, J. Smith, T. Stevens, W. Tasker, F. Taylor, T. Taylor, J. Thomas, J. Thompson, M. Tobin, P. Tobin, W.J. Todd, R. Tongue, J. Wall, A. Whetton, W. Wilcox, J. Williams (1395), J. Williams (934), J. Williams (1398), C. Wood

90th (Perthshire Volunteers) Light Infantry
Corporal J. Graham

Commissariat & Transport Department
Assistant Commissary W.A. Dunne
Acting Assist. Commissary J.L. Dalton
Acting storekeeper L.A. Byrne

Army Service Corps
Second Corporal F. Attwood

Army Medical Department
Surgeon Reynolds

Army Hospital Corps
Corporal R. Miller
Second Corporal McMahon
Private T. Luddington

Chaplain
The Reverend G. Smith

Natal Mounted Police
Troopers
R. Green, S. Hunter, H. Lugg

Natal Native Contingent
Lieutenant J. Adendorff

Corporals
M. Dougherty, J.H. Mayer, C. Scammell, C.F. Schiess, J. Wilson

Privates
One (name unknown)

Civilian
Mr Daniels (ferryman)

Note: a number of authenticated rolls of the Rorke's Drift garrison exist, and there are some discrepancies between them; for a discussion of their respective merits see Norman Holme's *The Silver Wreath*. It should also be noted that only some 95 men of the 2nd/24th were with B Coy.; the rest were patients in the hospital.

THE BRITISH PERIMETER, 22 JANUARY, 1630 HRS

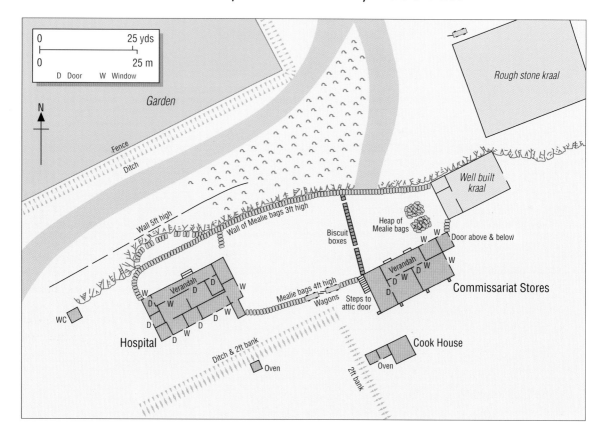

This was incorporated into the defensive line. A barricade of mealie-bags and biscuit-boxes was then run from the corner of the cattle-kraal right across the front of the post, to the far left corner of the hospital. Where possible this was placed on top of the ledge, so that three or four feet of barricade produced a barrier as much as eight feet high – a significant obstacle to a man attacking on foot. On the slope in front of the hospital, however, the barricade was less secure, and perhaps because it was the furthest point to which the heavy bags had to be dragged, it was not completed before the battle began; in some places it was shored up with pieces of planking. The two wagons were run into a line between the front left corner of the storehouse and the right rear of the hospital, and a line of biscuit-boxes was run between their wheels. These were covered over with mealie-bags to form a barricade four feet high, arguably the most secure one around the post.

It was impossible to include all the features of the post in the defensive line, however, and with no time to clear a field of fire, they were left for the enemy to take advantage of. A few yards beyond the back barricade there stood a small brick cook-house, and next to it two ovens, while at the front, below the cattle-kraal, was a rough animal pen made of piled stones. Chard's engineering equipment had been brought to the Drift in a mule-drawn General Service wagon, and this had been left close to the rough kraal. In front of the hospital was a fenced garden of fruit trees, and a half-completed wall lay at the foot of the slope. A patch of bush and long grass extended to within a few yards of the hospital veranda, punctuated here and there by isolated trees. All of this would, of course, provide excellent cover to any attackers.

Yet, despite the fact that the defenders felt themselves 'pinned like rats in a hole', the post was comparatively secure, given the sort of attack it could expect. The Zulus were, in effect, light infantry, who were capable of manoeuvring very rapidly, but were dependent on closing hand-to-hand to overwhelm their enemy. They had no artillery to knock down the defences, and the barricades would prevent them fighting effectively at close quarters. Their own encircling tactics could be highly effective in the open, but provided them no advantage against a position that was defended all round. Furthermore, although the Zulus were sure to outnumber the garrison heavily, the small size of the post meant that only part of their force could be brought into action at any given time. The dangers of attacking a prepared position defended with firearms had been well known in Zululand since a Zulu army had dashed itself to pieces on a Boer wagon-circle, in 1838, and King Cetshwayo had warned his men not to attack British strongholds – if they put their faces into the lair of a wild beast, he had told them, they would be sure to get clawed. It is to be wondered whether, in the coming fight, Prince Dabulamanzi regretted not having paid more attention to those words.

RIGHT *A war-shield of the uThulwana ibutho – white with red-brown patches – the principal Zulu regiment engaged at Rorke's Drift. (Africana Museum)*

FAR RIGHT *A Zulu shield apparently taken from the oNdini (Ulundi) ikhanda; if so, it must have been from the iNdluyengwe regiment, the youngest ibutho associated with the royal homestead, who are said to have carried black shields with white spots. (Africana Museum)*

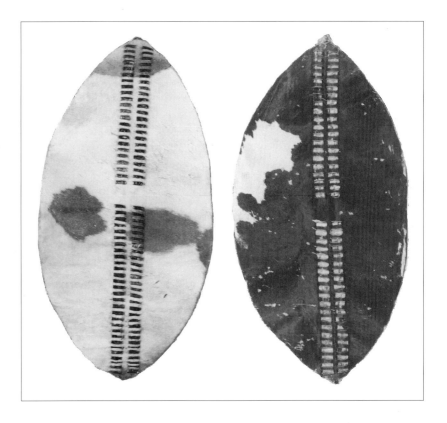

31

THE ZULUS

Unlike its British counterpart, the Zulu army was not a full-time professional body. Zulu men were required to give a period of service to their king, beginning when they were formed into regiments, called amabutho (sing. ibutho), at the age of about 19. Each ibutho was formed from men of a common age across the country, regardless of local origins or loyalties, and the amabutho system was a powerful centralising force within the kingdom. Once formed, each ibutho was required to spend several months each year living in the amakhanda, the king's royal homesteads, performing duties as varied as repairing the king's huts, taking part in royal hunts and serving as the state army.

This obligation to serve continued as long as the men were unmarried; marriage was an important rite of passage within Zulu society, and marked the point when a man fully came of age. It was acknowledged as a shift in an individual's responsibilities, away from a primary duty to serve the state and towards more immediate familial loyalties. When men married, they passed from active service into a reserve, and were only called out in times of national emergency. In effect, they were largely lost to the king as a resource, and as a result the Zulu kings artificially prolonged the state of bachelorhood, so that the men were seldom allowed to marry before they were 40 years old. The usual practice was for the king to grant permission for entire regiments to marry, and this change in status was recognised by the assumption of a ring of polished gum, the isicoco, worn stitched into the hair on top of the head.

Such was the perceived threat to the Zulu kingdom posed by the British advance that in January 1879 all regiments had been mustered, including the married ones. (Indeed, most of the men moving to attack Rorke's Drift were married.) The senior regiment among them, the uThulwana, comprised men in their mid-forties, and enjoyed a particularly high status within the kingdom. The king himself had served in the uThulwana in his youth, and it still included a great many of the important men of the nation. The uThulwana was unusual in that it was an *ibandla mhlope*, a 'white assembly' (so-called because married regiments usually carried white shields), a married regiment that still occasionally served in the amakhanda. It was quartered at oNdini itself, and the regiments that accompanied it were largely associated with the king's personal homestead. To maintain the regiment's size and prestige, the iNdlondlo, whose members were three or four years younger, had been incorporated into it, together with the iNdluyengwe. The iNdluyengwe men were in their late thirties and not yet married. The uDloko ibutho, also consisting of married men in their mid-forties, had also found themselves brigaded with the uThulwana in the confusion before Isandlwana. Although it was not necessary for a regiment to see action before it was allowed to marry, the older men had all seen action at the battle of 'Ndondakusuka, during the internal struggles of the 1850s, and in a number of skirmishes in the decades between.

On ceremonial occasions the amabutho paraded in the most magnificent costumes of feathered headresses and cow-tail body ornaments. Costumes varied from regiment to regiment, and served as an identifying uniform,

A Zulu induna, or state official, photographed shortly after the Anglo-Zulu War. Most of the men who attacked Rorke's Drift were of a similar age to this man, and wore the headring. (Africana Museum)

but they were too fragile and expensive to wear into battle. Most Zulu warriors went into action wearing nothing more than their loin-coverings – a thin belt of hide around the waist, with a square of dressed cowhide over the buttocks and strips of civet cat or monkey skin, twisted together to resemble tails, hanging down the front. A few might have retained padded headbands of otter or leopardskin, or perhaps arm and leg ornaments of cow-tails, while the izinduna may have worn single crane feathers or bunches of scarlet and green lourie feathers in their head-dresses as badges of their rank.

Most Zulu soldiers were armed with traditional weapons – the heavy, broad-bladed stabbing spear and a lighter spear for throwing. All would have carried oval war-shields of cow-hide; these shields were the property of the king, and were only issued to the warriors when they were on duty. The colours on the face of the hides were usually carefully matched, and reflected a broad distinction based on seniority; older regiments had white shields, younger ones black. The uThulwana and iNdlondlo carried white shields with small patches of red, while the unmarried iNdluyengwe still apparently carried black shields with large white patches on the bottom half. The uDloko carried either red-brown shields patterned with white, or white shields.

Generally the Zulu army had an essentially conservative military ethic, preferring to rely on fighting techniques that had proved consistently successful over the kingdom's 60-year history. Nevertheless, by 1879 many warriors carried firearms, and those on their way to attack Rorke's Drift were no exception. It is one of the myths of the battle that the Zulus first looted British firearms from the dead at Isandlwana, the reserve played no part in the battle, and the looting of the camp fell to those who had. In fact, a clandestine gun-trade had been operating in Zululand for almost 30 years. Guns were smuggled across the Natal border in small quantities, or more openly imported through Portuguese Mozambique in the north. Most of these weapons were obsolete patterns dumped on the unsophisticated world market by the European powers as weapon technology advanced rapidly in the 1830s and 1840s, and the majority of Zulus were armed with weapons as antiquated as the Brown Bess flintlock of the Napoleonic Wars. Nevertheless, more modern types were available, including the Enfield percussion rifle and a handful of sophisticated sporting guns. Shot was carried in a variety of improvised leather or canvas bags, and powder in cow-horns. Few Zulus understood the need to keep their weapons in good order, however, and even fewer traders sold good quality powder, ammunition or spares. Although a number of Zulus had been well trained by the many European hunters who had operated in the kingdom during the 1850s and 1860s, the majority had little idea how to get the best out of their weapons. Nevertheless, perhaps as many as two thirds of the Zulu army in 1879 had access to some sort of firearm.

Although a large number of the Zulus attacking at Rorke's Drift were armed with antiquated firearms, they still relied primarily on the traditional merits of the stabbing spear, such as these. (S.B. Bourquin)

OPPOSING COMMANDERS

THE BRITISH GARRISON

The battle of Rorke's Drift was no epic clash between great commanders with glittering reputations. Circumstances had thrown together a random assortment of men on either side; the most senior officers among the British were Lieutenants; not men who had been selected for their particular skill or courage, but simply those who were there on the day. They were typical products of their class and background, professional soldiers who had hitherto had no chance to shine, and might otherwise never have done so, while even the Zulu commander held no official appointment within the army. Fate brought them all together under desperate conditions on 22 January 1879, and the battle was to bring out the best in them all.

Neither Chard nor Bromhead had hitherto distinguished themselves in the eyes of their superiors. Chard was 31, from Devon, an experienced engineer who had nonetheless not seen action before. By all accounts he had a relaxed and affable personality, but was not a dynamic officer; as his superior put it, he was 'a most amiable fellow, and [an asset] to the mess, but as a company officer … hopelessly slow and slack'. Gonville 'Gunny' Bromhead, was 33, and had seen action on the Cape Frontier. He was quiet and reserved, perhaps as a result of impaired hearing. His fellow officers seem to have regarded him – unfairly – as rather slow, but 'as brave as a lion'. Indeed, after the war some officers, no doubt from jealousy, characterised both Chard and Bromhead as dull and stupid; but perhaps at Rorke's Drift a brilliant intellect was needed rather less than a dogged determination to hold one's ground, and that both men had in plenty.

Of the remaining officers, Assistant Commissary Dunne – whose rank was equivalent to lieutenant – had seen action on the Cape Frontier, as had his second-in-command, Dalton. Many of the survivors later credited Dalton with being the real hero of the battle – the man who conceived the defence, and whose courage and resolve throughout the fight was an inspiration to all. Of the Colonial officers, little is known. Adendorff is rather unfairly dismissed in some accounts as having fled before the battle started, but in fact all the evidence suggests he remained, and he deserves credit as the only man (on the British side) to have fought at both Isandlwana and Rorke's Drift. Captain Stevenson remains a shadowy figure, and he, very definitely, did not stay to take part in the fight.

The senior Commissariat officer present during the defence, Assistant Commissary Walter Dunne. (Author's collection)

34

THE ZULUS

The Zulu force approaching Rorke's Drift should have contained some of the most important personalities within the kingdom. The senior commanders of the uThulwana included Prince Hamu kaNzibe, the king's powerful half-brother, and Mnyamana Buthelezi, in his own right one of the most important chiefs within the kingdom and Cetshwayo's senior advisor. Yet Hamu had not taken to the field (indeed, he harboured secret plans to defect to the British), and Mnyamana was preoccupied with matters of state. Command of the uThulwana in the campaign seems to have devolved on Qethuka kaManqondo, a fiery and impetuous regimental officer who, despite the orders of the senior generals, had broken away from the reserve and led a section of his regiment in the attack on the camp at Isandlwana. The commander of the uDloko was Zibhebhu kaMapitha, another powerful chieftain in his own right, and arguably the best general to emerge from the 1879 war; yet Zibhebhu too had taken part in the attack on the camp, and had been wounded in the hand during the pursuit. No doubt recalling the king's prohibition on crossing the river, he had taken the opportunity to retire from the field.

The man whom many present felt was the real power behind the defence; Acting Assistant Commissary James Langley Dalton. (Royal Archives)

The only commander of any importance left with the reserve was Prince Dabulamanzi kaMpande. An aggressive man about 40 years of age, who was well known to Natal traders for his sharp mind and truculent manner, Dabulamanzi was a good shot and an able horseman, but he was regarded by his colleagues as being too headstrong. Perhaps because of this, he held no official appointment in the army. He commanded the reserve simply by virtue of his powerful personality and his position as an *umntwana* – a royal prince. The decision to cross the river, and to attack Rorke's Drift without having first made any serious plans, was typical of his character.

Of the remaining izinduna, little is known. At least one other senior commander was present, and each regiment included a compliment of colonels and junior commanders, yet their names have gone unrecorded, both in British sources and in Zulu history. It is a curious feature of the battle that while so much is known about the individuals who made up the British side, next to nothing is known about those who faced them.

Prince Dabulamanzi kaMpande and his adherents in 1873. Dabulamanzi was a noted shot, and this picture gives a good impression of the sort of firearms with which the Zulus were armed. The prince and his standing attendants have good-quality hunting guns, but the remainder of the party have older percussion and flintlock models. (Killie Campbell Africana Library)

THE BATTLE OF RORKE'S DRIFT

THE ZULU APPROACH

At about 4.00pm, while the garrison was working feverishly to complete the barricades, a party of about 100 black horsemen under a white officer rode up to the post. These were Natal Native Horse survivors of Isandlwana, who had cut their way through the encircling Zulu horns, and they now offered their services to Chard, who was delighted to accept. He asked them to spread out in a screen beyond the Shiyane hill, to try to slow the enemy advance. They had not been gone long, however, when the garrison heard a smatter of shots, and the horsemen came into view again, this time streaming past on the road to Helpmekaar. A civilian with them called out a warning: 'Here they come, black as hell and thick as grass!', while their officer reined in long enough to apologise that his men would not obey him, before he too rode on. Even Chard found it difficult to blame them; they had performed well at Isandlwana, but they were exhausted, their ammunition was gone, and they were badly shaken by the events they had witnessed earlier in the day.

Their departure caused a much more serious defection, however. Stevenson's NNC company took one look at them and decided to follow their example, throwing down their weapons, vaulting over the barricades and fleeing into the bush. B Company were particularly infuriated by the sight of their white NCOs and officers going with them, and fired a few shots after them, dropping one of the white NCOs in front of the hospital. In a matter of minutes Chard's position had deteriorated badly; he had counted on between 300 and 400 men to man a perimeter which stretched for more than 100 yards and included two buildings, and now he had just 150. As a precaution he immediately gave the order to build a new barricade, a row of biscuit-boxes, stacked two high, which bisected the yard, running from the front left corner of the storehouse to the front barricade. Gaps were left for the men to move through, but the position was now effectively cut in half, so that if either building fell, it would be possible to fall back on the other. This line was scarcely complete when a shout from a lookout posted on the hospital roof warned that the Zulus were approaching. Just before they came into view, the Reverend Witt decided that a battle was no place for a Christian missionary, and he rode off to Helpmekaar; his colleague Chaplain Smith might have joined him, but

The battlefield today, showing the line of the back wall (marked by stones in the grass), looking towards the Church, which was built on the site of the old storehouse. The two wagons were built into this line, and it was against this that the first Zulu attack was directed. (Author's photo)

found someone had stolen his horse, and resolved instead to stay and offer what assistance he could. It was now about 4.30pm.

The Zulus had made a leisurely approach. The iNdluyengwe had crossed the river where it flowed through a narrow fissure in the rocks half a mile upstream from Sothondose's Drift, and had paused on the hills on the Natal bank to recover and take snuff. An hour earlier the observers on the Shiyane hill had seen the older amabutho cross much closer to Rorke's Drift, at a spot where the river was wide but only waist-deep; the Zulus had formed a human chain and passed one another across before they too had paused to dry out and take snuff. Of the 6,000 men who had formed the reserve in the morning, a number had already broken away. Some sections of the uThulwana had taken part in the attack on Isandlwana, while a number of iNdluyengwe had lingered to hunt down fugitives hiding in the bush and caves overlooking the river. Once across, elements from both groups peeled off to ransack the deserted African homesteads and a solitary European farm which lay between Sothondose's and Rorke's Drift. Some pushed even further afield, and there are suggestions that some even reached the foot of the Helpmekaar heights. In all, there were between 3,000 and 4,000 left in the main bodies.

When the senior amabutho moved off, they divided in two; one section apparently intended to move round Shiyane to the north, on the river side, but thought better of it and returned to join the other. The iNdluyengwe's line of advance took them ahead of the senior party, and from the storehouse the garrison's lookout could see them on the southern flank of Shiyane, halting under the shelter of a slight rise. They deployed in a line, screened with skirmishers in open order, then advanced rapidly to attack, fanning out into their usual crescent attack formation.

There were perhaps 500 or 600 of the iNdluyengwe in this first rush, and they came within sight of the garrison at about 600 yards' range. They were in open order, the warriors crouching low, running from cover to

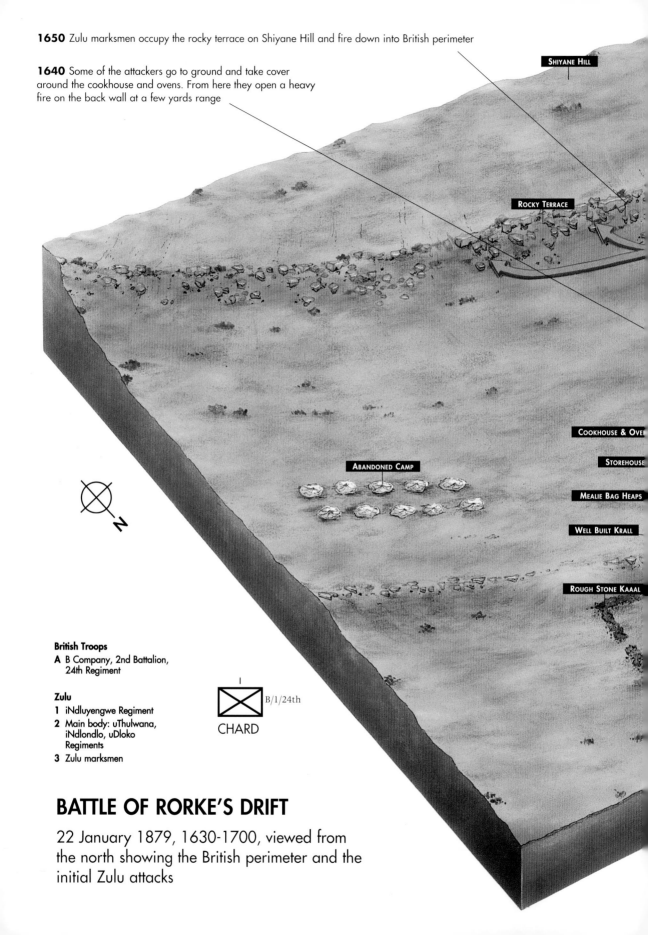

1650 Zulu marksmen occupy the rocky terrace on Shiyane Hill and fire down into British perimeter

1640 Some of the attackers go to ground and take cover around the cookhouse and ovens. From here they open a heavy fire on the back wall at a few yards range

SHIYANE HILL

ROCKY TERRACE

COOKHOUSE & OVEN

STOREHOUSE

ABANDONED CAMP

MEALIE BAG HEAPS

WELL BUILT KRAAL

ROUGH STONE KAAAL

British Troops
A B Company, 2nd Battalion, 24th Regiment

Zulu
1 iNdluyengwe Regiment
2 Main body: uThulwana, iNdlondlo, uDloko Regiments
3 Zulu marksmen

B/1/24th
CHARD

BATTLE OF RORKE'S DRIFT

22 January 1879, 1630-1700, viewed from the north showing the British perimeter and the initial Zulu attacks

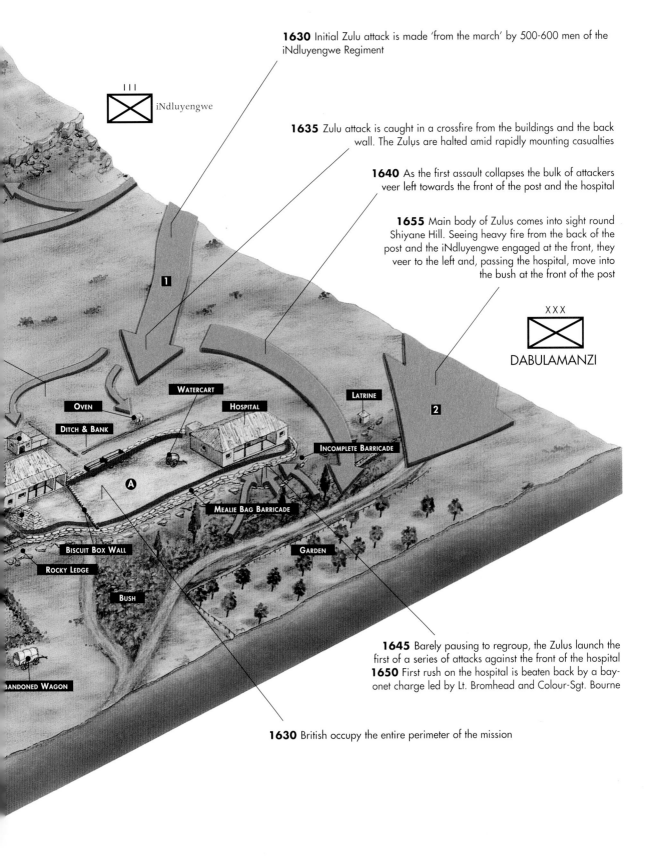

1630 Initial Zulu attack is made 'from the march' by 500-600 men of the iNdluyengwe Regiment

iNdluyengwe

1635 Zulu attack is caught in a crossfire from the buildings and the back wall. The Zulus are halted amid rapidly mounting casualties

1640 As the first assault collapses the bulk of attackers veer left towards the front of the post and the hospital

1655 Main body of Zulus comes into sight round Shiyane Hill. Seeing heavy fire from the back of the post and the iNdluyengwe engaged at the front, they veer to the left and, passing the hospital, move into the bush at the front of the post

DABULAMANZI

OVEN

WATERCART

HOSPITAL

LATRINE

DITCH & BANK

INCOMPLETE BARRICADE

A

MEALIE BAG BARRICADE

BISCUIT BOX WALL

GARDEN

ROCKY LEDGE

BUSH

1645 Barely pausing to regroup, the Zulus launch the first of a series of attacks against the front of the hospital
1650 First rush on the hospital is beaten back by a bayonet charge led by Lt. Bromhead and Colour-Sgt. Bourne

ABANDONED WAGON

1630 British occupy the entire perimeter of the mission

cover with their shields held out in front of them. Chard gave the order to fire at about 500 yards' range, and commented that the shooting was a little unsteady at first, but that by the time the Zulus had closed to within 450 yards the men were firing coolly and accurately. Several of the garrison recalled afterwards that the Zulus would spring in the air and somersault backwards as they were struck, no doubt as a result of the impact of the heavy Martini-Henry bullets. Nevertheless, the attack did not waver until it pressed close to the buildings, and Chard thought for a moment that 'nothing would stop them'. However, at just 50 yards from the rear wall they were caught in a heavy crossfire from the buildings, and the attack stalled. Large numbers of warriors threw themselves down in the grass and wriggled forward to take possession of the cover offered by the cook-house and ovens. From here they opened a heavy fire on the back wall at just a few yards' range.

Checked at the rear of the post, most of the iNdluyengwe veered to their left, passed round the end of the hospital, and poured into the bush at the front of the post. From here, scarcely pausing to regroup, they launched the first of a series of attacks on the front of the hospital, and it immediately became apparent that this was the post's weak-spot. The Zulus were able to advance under the shelter of long grass and bush almost to the foot of the slope, then only had to run a few feet across the open to reach the inadequate barricade. Despite a heavy fire poured into them at close range, they rushed right up and engaged the defenders hand to hand. It was here that members of the garrison first noticed a distinctive feature of the fight; the Zulus paid no attention to the rifle fire whatsoever, and it was only when the bayonet was used freely that they 'flinched the least bit'. According to Private Fred Hitch of B Company, 'Had the Zulus taken the bayonet as freely as they took the bullets, we could not have stood more than fifteen minutes.' No doubt the bayonet was indeed a formidable weapon, outreaching the Zulu stabbing spear by an arm's length, but the Zulu disregard for bullets probably owed as much to their pre-battle rituals, which encouraged them to believe that the soldiers' bullets would not

Witt's house today; the original hospital had a similar appearance, but a thatched roof. The incomplete mealie-bag barricades ran across the veranda in the foreground; it was across this sloping ground that the Zulus charged repeatedly at the beginning of the battle. (Author's photo)

harm them. For whatever reason, this first rush was driven back by a
squad of men in a bayonet charge led by Lieutenant Bromhead and Colour-
Sergeant Bourne.

THE MAIN ATTACK

The first rush on the hospital had just been beaten back when the main
Zulu body – the uThulwana, iNdlondlo and uDloko – came into sight
round the hill. Seeing the heavy fire from the back of the post, and that
the iNdluyengwe were already engaged at the front, this body veered
slightly to its left, passed the hospital and moved into the bush at the front
in a dense mass. They were apparently led by two izinduna on horseback;
one, whose name is not recorded, was shot dead by a soldier on the back
wall, and the other was Prince Dabulamanzi. Although the attack so far
showed no signs of careful planning – the Zulus had simply advanced and
attacked – a directing hand became more obvious once the Prince arrived.
Little is known of the battle from his perspective, however, and it is left
to the historian to explore his reasoning from the evidence of the subsequent Zulu movements. Nor is it known where the Prince stood during the
fight, although there is a local story that he took up a position on the
shoulder of the hill overlooking the post, below the line of broken strata,
and this would have been entirely in keeping with the Zulu practice of
commanding battles from an elevated vantage point.

Once the main body had manoeuvred into position, the attacks on the
hospital veranda were renewed with heightened intensity. Several times

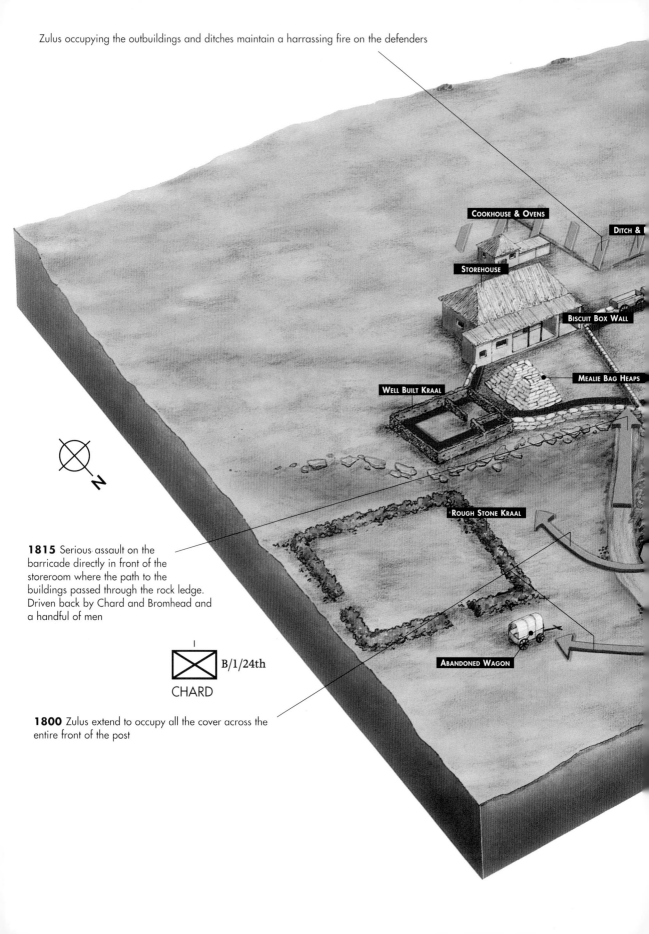

Zulus occupying the outbuildings and ditches maintain a harrassing fire on the defenders

COOKHOUSE & OVENS

DITCH & [

STOREHOUSE

BISCUIT BOX WALL

MEALIE BAG HEAPS

WELL BUILT KRAAL

ROUGH STONE KRAAL

N

1815 Serious assault on the barricade directly in front of the storeroom where the path to the buildings passed through the rock ledge. Driven back by Chard and Bromhead and a handful of men

B/1/24th

CHARD

ABANDONED WAGON

1800 Zulus extend to occupy all the cover across the entire front of the post

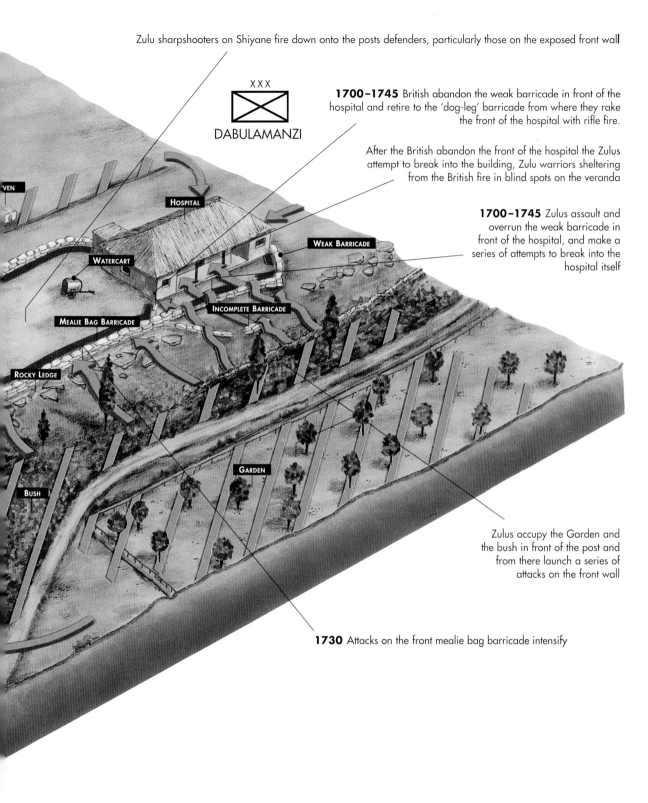

Zulu sharpshooters on Shiyane fire down onto the posts defenders, particularly those on the exposed front wall

XXX

DABULAMANZI

1700–1745 British abandon the weak barricade in front of the hospital and retire to the 'dog-leg' barricade from where they rake the front of the hospital with rifle fire.

After the British abandon the front of the hospital the Zulus attempt to break into the building, Zulu warriors sheltering from the British fire in blind spots on the veranda

1700–1745 Zulus assault and overrun the weak barricade in front of the hospital, and make a series of attempts to break into the hospital itself

VEN

HOSPITAL

WATERCART

WEAK BARRICADE

INCOMPLETE BARRICADE

MEALIE BAG BARRICADE

ROCKY LEDGE

BUSH

GARDEN

Zulus occupy the Garden and the bush in front of the post and from there launch a series of attacks on the front wall

1730 Attacks on the front mealie bag barricade intensify

BATTLE OF RORKE'S DRIFT

22 January 1879, 1700–1815, viewed from north showing the main Zulu attacks and the assault on the hospital

A mark on the lip of the rocky ledge, believed to have been caused by a Martini-Henry bullet aimed at Zulus crouching below. (Author's photo)

The ferocity of the Zulu attacks on the front barricade, coupled with the casualties caused by fire from the Shiyane hill, finally forced Chard to abandon the yard at about 6.00pm. (Author's collection)

the warriors rose up out of the cover and charged forward, shouting the war-cry 'Usuthu!', only to be driven back after a violent melee that spilled onto the veranda itself. At such close range, the British fire was devastating, and the area in front of the building was soon carpeted with dead and dying Zulus. Others took advantage of the bush to extend their attacks further to their left, trying to find a way in along the centre of the front barricade. The combination of rocky ledge and barricade was too much of an obstacle, however, and they were shot down or bayoneted as they tried to clamber up.

With the arrival of the main body the Zulus also moved to occupy the Shiyane terrace. A line of sandstone ran around the foot of the hill, and where it was exposed to the elements, great slabs of rock had broken off and fallen away, forming a jumble of boulders, pitted in between with shallow caves and crevices. It was excellent natural cover, and hundreds of Zulus armed with firearms nestled in among the rocks and opened a heavy fire on the back of the post. Although the buildings themselves obscured part of the perimeter, the Zulu marksmen had an uninterrupted view into the yard between, and the men manning the front barricade – whose backs were exposed to the hill – were particularly vulnerable to their fire. Chard could do little but order the men on the back barricade, who were comparatively safe, to suppress the Zulu fire as best as they could.

In this they were at a distinct advantage. Although the Zulu position was a commanding one – a squad of good shots armed with efficient rifles could have made Chard's position untenable within minutes – the Zulus were neither good shots nor well armed. The old Brown Bess, probably the single most common firearm among them, had been designed for use against mass targets at ranges of little more than 100 yards, and the distance to the front wall was at least three times that. Although this range was better suited to more modern percussion rifles, which were also pre-

Corporal Allen of B Company – promoted to sergeant, and wearing his VC at the end of the war. Allen was wounded in the arm by fire from Shiyane early in the fight, but continued to serve out ammunition throughout the night. (Royal Archives)

Louis Byrne, a civilian volunteer serving with the Commissary Department. Byrne was handing a cup of water to the wounded Corporal Scammell of the NNC when he was struck through the head and killed by a bullet fired from Shiyane hill. (Author's collection)

sent in significant numbers, the Zulus were still hampered by poor quality powder and inferior ammunition. Proper musket balls were always in short supply, and many Zulus made their own, either in crude moulds or from likely substitutes including pebbles and irregular-shaped pieces of iron. These projectiles made a terrifying noise in flight, and could inflict horrific wounds at short range, but their trajectory was so erratic that aimed fire at anything more than 50 or 60 yards away was pointless. Although a tremendous volume of shot struck down into the British position, it did so almost at random, and any casualties were inflicted more by luck than judgement. Furthermore, it was by now late afternoon, on a clear day, and the evening sun, setting behind the Helpmekaar heights, shone directly onto the slopes of Shiyane, and into the eyes of the marksmen, making their task even more difficult.

For the British, however, the situation was reversed; the sun lit up the Zulu positions like a search-light, and the position of even the most carefully concealed sniper was revealed by the quantities of smoke belching out from their old black powder weapons. The range of 300-400 yards was an ideal one for the Martini-Henry, and the barricade offered them an opportunity to rest their weapons and pick their shots carefully. The line on the back wall, apparently under the command of Sergeant Gallagher of B Company, seems to have included a number of the best shots in the company, and one man, Private Dunbar, dropped nine Zulus in as many shots.

Nevertheless, the Zulu fire was dangerous. Corporal Lyons on the back wall leaned forward over the barricade to get a better aim, and was struck high in the shoulder by a musket ball which lodged in his spine. His friend Corporal Allen went to attend to him, and Allen too was hit in the arm. On the front barricade James Dalton was also hit, though whether from the hill or from a shot fired from the bush at the front of the post is not clear. Dalton had already played an active part in the defence. During the struggle in front of the hospital he had shot a Zulu who was in the very act of spearing a man of the Army Hospital Corps. He had been firing over the barricade when a Zulu ran up close to it, unscathed. Dalton called out, 'Pot that fellow' (someone did), then suddenly stiffened and stood upright. As he turned Chard noticed that he had been hit by a bullet which had passed through him near the shoulder. He was taken off to Surgeon Reynolds for treatment. A corporal in the Natal Native Contingent, Scammell, was shot through the shoulder and carried off to the veranda of the storehouse, where Reynolds had established a makeshift dressing-station. Scammell recovered sufficiently to notice that Chard was using a Martini-Henry over the front barricade. Being an officer and having no rifle ammunition pouches, Chard was looking around for cartridges, and Scammell crawled across to hand him his. The effort exhausted the corporal, however, who slumped against the barricade calling for water. The storekeeper, Louis Byrne, fetched him a cup from a two-wheeled water-cart which had been left in the centre of the yard, but as he bent forward to hand it to Scammell, Byrne was struck through the head by a bullet from the hill and killed instantly.

The battle had now been raging for perhaps an hour, and the incidence of these casualties was causing Chard some concern. The attacks on the

From their positions in the shallow caves and crevices on the slopes of Shiyane hill, Zulu marksmen were able to fire right down into the British defensive position. Chard's men on the front barricade, who had their backs to the hill, were particularly vulnerable to this fire, but the range – about 300 yards – was too great for the obsolete flintlocks and percussion rifles carried by the Zulus to be very effective. British return fire was more accurate. This is the scene at about 5.00pm, with the Zulu attack on the back of the post pinned down, but heavy fighting ranging along the front of the hospital. (Michael Perry)

front wall showed no signs of abating; indeed, the defenders had finally been driven off the veranda, and had retired to an improvised dog-leg barricade which connected the front right corner of the hospital to the front wall. From here they could rake the front of the hospital with rifle fire, although dozens of warriors pressed themselves against the walls in the sheltered blind-spots and tried to batter their way in through the front doors. Furthermore, the attacks along the centre of the front wall were now even more determined. A serious assault took place on the barricade directly in front of the storehouse. A track ran up to the buildings there, through the ledge, and although it had been blocked off with mealie-bags, it provided less of an obstacle to the attackers. Chard gathered two or three men to meet the rush, and was joined by Bromhead with two or three more. It was repulsed, but Chard was concerned that his mounting casualties in the yard might leave a section of the wall undefended, and allow a Zulu breakthrough. At about 6.00pm he gave the order for his men to

The rocky ledge along the front of the post provided a formidable barrier against the Zulu attack, especially when topped by a mealie-bag barricade. Once Chard abandoned the yard, however, the Zulus were able to crouch in the dead ground below the rocks, and spring up to fire at the defenders at close range. (Author's photos)

abandon the yard and retreat back behind the interior partition of biscuit-boxes. The retreat seems to have been carried out quickly and in good order. The wounded were dragged inside the new perimeter, but there was no time to carry away the dead; they were left where they had fallen.

The new position offered Chard a number of advantages. It was almost entirely protected from fire from the hill by the storehouse, so the Zulu marksmen were deprived of their targets; he had the same number of men to defend a much smaller area, and his line was therefore more compact; and the fire from the biscuit-box wall made it impossible for the Zulus to force a way into the yard, while that from the loopholes in the storehouse kept them away from the rear wall. It did mean, however, that the Zulus could now rush forward and occupy the area at the foot of the old front wall, which, even at such short range, was effectively dead ground. Here dozens of them could mass, untouched by British fire until they sprang up to rush forward or tried to clamber over the barricade. Worse still, it meant that it was impossible to keep them away from the hospital, which was now an isolated bastion, defended only by its patients and a handful of able-bodied men, in the midst of ground occupied by the enemy.

THE FIGHT FOR THE HOSPITAL

The fight for the hospital is one of the most famous incidents of the battle, yet it is difficult to reconstruct the events which took place there with any real certainty. Only one of the defenders left a detailed account, and

Private Alfred Henry Hook of B Company, who earned the VC for his part in the defence of the hospital. (Keith Reeves collection)

RIGHT *The Zulus repeatedly attacked the doors and windows of the hospital building, at last forcing the defenders to retreat room by room. (Author's collection)*

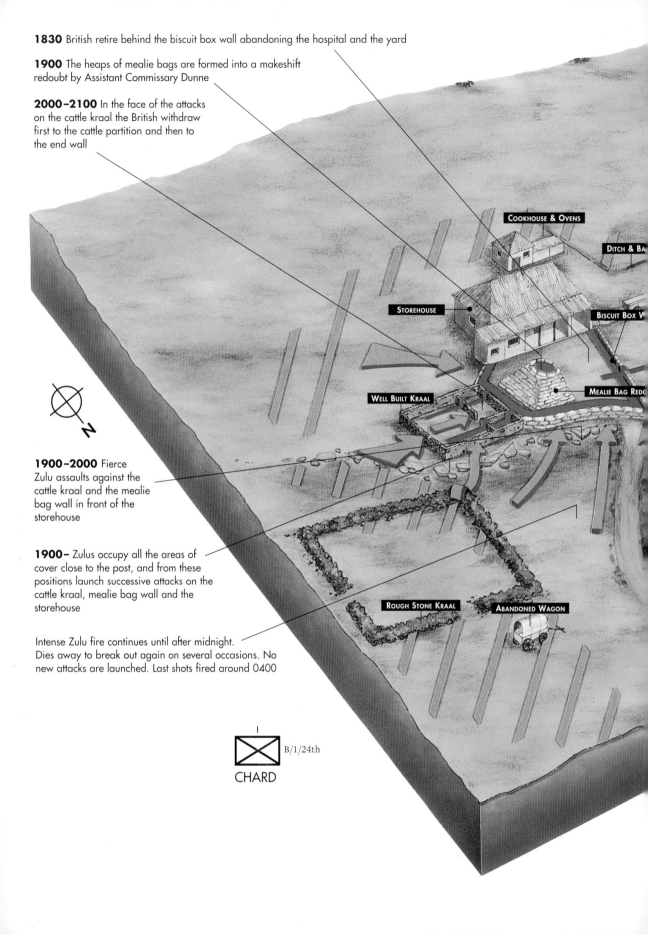

1830 British retire behind the biscuit box wall abandoning the hospital and the yard

1900 The heaps of mealie bags are formed into a makeshift redoubt by Assistant Commissary Dunne

2000–2100 In the face of the attacks on the cattle kraal the British withdraw first to the cattle partition and then to the end wall

1900–2000 Fierce Zulu assaults against the cattle kraal and the mealie bag wall in front of the storehouse

1900– Zulus occupy all the areas of cover close to the post, and from these positions launch successive attacks on the cattle kraal, mealie bag wall and the storehouse

Intense Zulu fire continues until after midnight. Dies away to break out again on several occasions. No new attacks are launched. Last shots fired around 0400

COOKHOUSE & OVENS

DITCH & BA

STOREHOUSE

BISCUIT BOX V

MEALIE BAG REDC

WELL BUILT KRAAL

ROUGH STONE KRAAL

ABANDONED WAGON

N

B/1/24th

CHARD

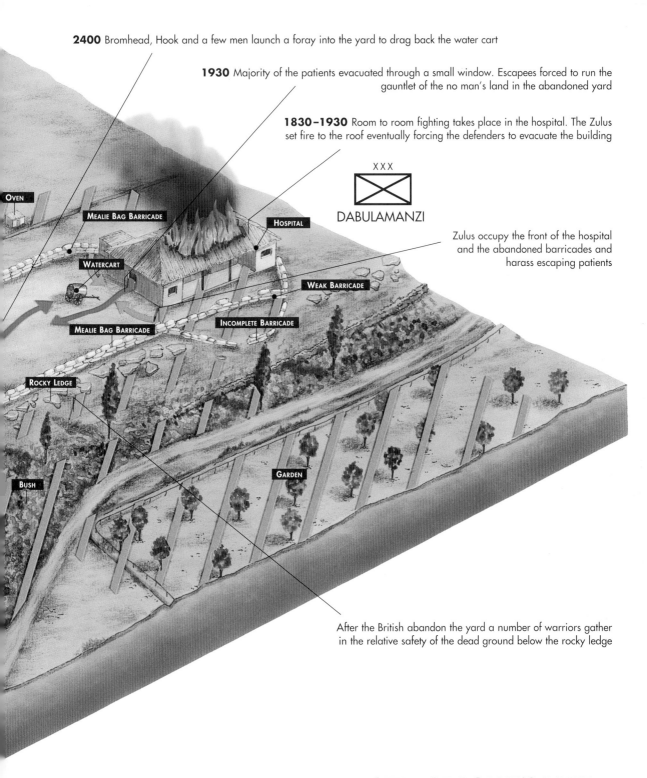

2400 Bromhead, Hook and a few men launch a foray into the yard to drag back the water cart

1930 Majority of the patients evacuated through a small window. Escapees forced to run the gauntlet of the no man's land in the abandoned yard

1830-1930 Room to room fighting takes place in the hospital. The Zulus set fire to the roof eventually forcing the defenders to evacuate the building

x x x

DABULAMANZI

Zulus occupy the front of the hospital and the abandoned barricades and harass escaping patients

OVEN

MEALIE BAG BARRICADE

HOSPITAL

WATERCART

WEAK BARRICADE

MEALIE BAG BARRICADE

INCOMPLETE BARRICADE

ROCKY LEDGE

GARDEN

BUSH

After the British abandon the yard a number of warriors gather in the relative safety of the dead ground below the rocky ledge

BATTLE OF RORKE'S DRIFT

22 January 1879, 1815–2400, viewed from north showing the later Zulu attacks and the British withdrawal to the final perimeter

that was written years afterwards, when the overall impression must inevitably have remained more vivid than the precise details of the sequence and location of events. Indeed, some of the most terrible struggles in that dark warren of little rooms undoubtedly left no British observers alive to record them, and there is an almost total absence of evidence from Zulu sources. Tempting as it is to try, it is not possible to describe the precise movements of individual participants with any certainty.

According to one of the defenders, Private Henry Hook, 'To talk of a hospital gives the idea of a big building, but as a matter of fact this hospital was a mere little shed or bungalow, divided up into rooms so small you could hardly swing a bayonet in them.' It was hardly ideal ground to fight on. The patients had been placed on improvised beds made by raising planks a few inches off the bare floor. Only a handful were still lying helpless on them, but as it grew dark each room must have been gloomy, claustrophobic and littered with obstacles to hamper movement. The doors and windows had been sealed off with biscuit-boxes and mealie-bags, and the building had remained secure during the first rush. The defenders – six able-bodied men and perhaps 20 armed patients – had a good field of fire from behind windows and loop-holes, but the Zulus came on in such numbers that they were at last able to get close enough to run right up to the outside walls. Pressing themselves flat against them, they grabbed at the rifles as they poked through, spoiling the aim and trying to tear off the bayonets, or tried to thrust their own firearms into the loopholes. They broke in first through a door in the wall on the western end of the building, where a defender, Private Joseph Williams, apparently succeeded in shooting 14 of them before he was overcome. The details of Williams' death are unclear, since he appears to have fallen outside the building. He may have been trying to lean out of his position to get a better aim, or perhaps had simply decided he could no longer remain where he was. In any case, a Zulu managed to grab hold of him and pull him out through the door, where he was set upon and speared to death. At the front too, once the dog-leg barricade had been abandoned, there was nothing to stop the Zulus rushing the veranda, and forcing their way in through the doors at the front. It is possible that two or three patients were overrun and killed in the rooms on this side.

Such were the conditions, however, that most of the defenders were unaware of what was happening outside their own rooms. The sound of Martini-Henry fire echoed and boomed around the walls, and there was a constant roar from outside, where the steady crackle of musket-fire, the cries of the wounded and the rattle of weapons blended with the deeper roar of the war-cry 'Usuthu!'. No sooner had the Zulus reached the building than they set the roof on fire. The thatch was damp from days of intermittent rain, but the rooms gradually filled with a dense, choking smoke.

Private Hook recalled that he had been posted in a room overlooking the hill together with a Private Cole, inevitably known to his friends as 'Old King'. There was just one patient in the room, an auxiliary from the NNC who had been wounded in the action at Sihayo's stronghold, and whose leg was so heavily bandaged that he could not move. The battle had

Private Hook, defending a loop-hole in one of the cramped rooms inside the hospital. (Author's collection)

Private John Williams VC, one of the defenders of the hospital. (Keith Reeves collection)

52

While one man keeps the Zulus at bay, others help the patients away through holes hastily knocked in the flimsy interior walls. (Author's collection)

The desperate struggle inside the dark and claustrophobic hospital rooms is vividly captured in this contemporary illustration. (Author's collection)

no sooner begun than Cole declared he could stand the cramped conditions no longer, and went outside; he emerged onto the veranda during one of the Zulu attacks, and was promptly shot dead. The patient in Hook's room called out for him to take off the bandages, but Hook found it 'impossible to do anything but fight, and I blazed away as hard as I could'. Hook's room was connected to another by a flimsy interior door, and when it became too full of smoke for him to bear, he rushed through. He was unable to take the patient with him, and years later he recalled the sound of tearing bandages as the Zulus broke in and the man attempted to escape.

Hook was now in a room containing several patients. The Zulus were trying to break through the door he had shut behind him, and everyone who was able fired away or jabbed at them with their bayonets. Suddenly above the din Hook heard Private John Williams shout out, 'The Zulus are swarming all over the place. They've dragged Joseph Williams out and killed him.' The two Williams were not related; John Williams had apparently been in another room when the Zulus burst in, and had taken advantage of Joseph Williams' last struggle to quickly knock a hole through one of the interior walls, emerging into the room where Hook was now fighting. This room, however, had no door in it beside the one through which Hook had entered, and the only chance for escape seemed to be to follow Williams' example. Fortunately, although the outside walls of the building were made of brick and stone, the interior walls were made of sun-dried mud-brick. As Hook put it, 'These shoddy inside bricks proved our salvation.' The defenders had at least one pick-axe with them – they had brought it to make loop-holes – and together with their bayonets they used it to hack at the wall. While this was going on at least one man had to hold back the Zulus, which was dangerous work, Hook himself was struck on the head by a flung spear which, had it not been

Alphonse de Neuville's famous painting of the battle, which captures the overall scene very well, but telescopes several incidents into one moment. In the centre Surgeon Reynolds tends the wounded Dalton, with Bromhead, pointing, behind him. Chaplain Smith hands out ammunition, while Corporal Scammell of the NNC – here incorrectly shown in the uniform of the 24th – hands cartridges to Chard, and bullets from Shiyane strike down into the yard. In fact the hospital was not evacuated as shown until after Chard had abandoned the yard. (RRW Museum, Brecon)

Private Robert Jones VC, a hospital defender.

deflected by the peak of his helmet, might have caused serious injury. When the hole was big enough, the patients were pushed and pulled through one by one, until at last the man defending the room sprinted after them. Then the whole process began anew in the next room.

While this deadly game of cat and mouse was going on through the rooms at the back of the hospital, a number of defenders elsewhere in the building escaped as best they could. In one, two privates, Beckett and Waters, had defended themselves from the cover of a large wardrobe belonging to Mr Witt. Waters had been wounded twice, but between them they had killed several Zulus, whose bodies now lay on the floor in front of the wardrobe. Miraculously they were not discovered. As the room filled with smoke from the burning roof, however, the tension became unbearable, and Beckett resolved to slip away. He dashed out of the room and across the veranda, presumably hoping to throw himself down in the cover beyond the front of the post; unfortunately he blundered into a Zulu, who stabbed him through the stomach as he passed, and Beckett managed only a few more steps before he collapsed into the long grass. Waters, meanwhile, stayed inside for as long as he dared, and then fled wrapped in one of the Reverend Witt's long black cloaks that he had found in the wardrobe. It was dark by this time, and the Zulus were no doubt distracted by the fighting around the storehouse. Waters crept round the side of the hospital unnoticed, and worked towards the cook-house at the back of the post. This was only a few yards away from the storehouse, and no doubt

he hoped to be able to reach Chard's new position. When he entered the cook-house, to his horror he found it full of Zulus engaged in firing at the garrison. They did not notice him enter behind them, however. Waters reached out and grabbed a handful of soot from the ovens, which he smeared over his face and hands, and then crouched down in the shadows, covering himself with his cloak. Astonishingly he was never spotted, and he survived to rejoin the garrison the next morning. Nor was he the only man to do so. Indeed the number of British soldiers who survived the night

Private William Jones VC, another of the hospital defenders. (Royal Archives)

Once the men had withdrawn behind the biscuit-box wall, the front corner, where it abutted the barricade, became particularly dangerous, as it was exposed to Zulu fire from several directions. Private Nicholas was shot through the head and killed, whilst Private Hitch was hit in the shoulder by a ball which smashed his shoulder blade. A friend bound Hitch's wound with cloth from the lining of a coat, and Hitch continued to fight, armed with Lieutenant Bromhead's revolver; Bromhead himself commanded this corner, firing over the barricade with a rifle. (Michael Perry)

outside the perimeter seems positively bizarre. Gunner Howard RA, one of the patients, also fled out into the darkness, and hid among the bush at the front of the post. Several times during the night the Zulus trod on him, but they must have thought him the body of one of their own companions, as none stopped to examine him.

In the hospital, meanwhile, Hook and his party had worked their way through to the rooms at the eastern end of the building. At one point a private named Connolly, who had a broken thigh-bone and was too large to fit comfortably through the holes, had to be dragged through forcibly. 'His leg got broken again,' admitted Hook, 'but there was no help for it.'

After the yard had been abandoned, this angle – between the line of biscuit-boxes and the front barricade – became one of the most dangerous on the post. Exposed to a galling cross-fire, it was here that Private Hitch was wounded. (Author's photo)

Chaplain George Smith, the Central Column's unofficial chaplain, who stayed to assist in the defence, handing out ammunition with the exhortation: 'Don't swear boys, and shoot them!' (Nottingham Castle collection)

Curiously, Connolly too opted to take his chances out in the darkness on his own, rather than try to get back to Chard's redoubt. Waiting for a quiet moment, he pulled himself up on some mealie-bags, squeezed out through a window, then, unable to walk, pushed himself forward with his hands, feet first. Remarkably he too survived.

The remaining patients faced an equally terrifying ordeal. The only way out of the building was now through a small window which opened into the centre of the yard. But the yard had now been abandoned, and was effectively no-man's land. The defenders had to pass the patients out into the darkness, where they dropped to the ground and had to scramble as best they could across the yard towards the sanctuary of the biscuit-box wall opposite. Although fire from that barricade kept the yard free of Zulus, the warriors nonetheless crouched along the veranda and behind parts of the front wall, firing and throwing spears at short range. Not everyone made it. Trooper Hunter of the Natal Mounted Police was confused for a second or two as he emerged from the window, dazzled by the glare from the burning roof and the noise. As he stood looking which way to run, a particularly bold warrior sprinted across the open and speared him through the kidneys. The Zulu was shot dead seconds later, but Hunter was killed. Another man, Sergeant Maxfield of the 24th, was lying delirious in his bed, and had struggled with his rescuers so much that they had left him till last; when they went back for him, they were too late, and

watched in horror as the Zulus burst into the room and killed him. Yet, for the most part, the majority of the patients made it across the exposed area safely, and eager hands helped them behind the barricade.

THE FIGHTING AROUND THE STOREHOUSE

Even as the desperate struggle in the hospital was under way, the Zulus kept up their pressure on the storehouse. A number of attacks had risen up out of the bush and dashed themselves against the front barricade, and although they had been repulsed, it soon became clear that the angle between the front wall and the line of biscuit-boxes was now the most vulnerable sector of the perimeter. This area was the least sheltered from the fire directed on the post from all directions. Furthermore, the Zulus could creep up under cover of the rocky ledge and crouch almost below it with impunity. From here they would spring up and fire at the defenders as they showed themselves over the mealie-bags above. Bromhead himself took command of this sector, but the fire was so dangerous that of six men with him only he and one other escaped injury. Private Nicholas was shot through the head at this time, his brains spattering his companions. Another of those hit was probably Corporal Schiess, an NCO of the NNC who hailed from Switzerland. Schiess had been a patient in the hospital, suffering from severe blisters, but had taken his place on the wall, and about this time had been struck in the foot by a bullet which tore open his instep. According to Chard, Schiess determined to clear the Zulus away from the ledge, and leaving the shelter of the biscuit-box wall, he crept out a few yards along the abandoned front barricade, suddenly stood up,

The rocky ledge along the front of the post, whilst it gave the defenders a vital height advantage, provided dead ground where the Zulus could concentrate once Chard had withdrawn from part of the barricade. In a famous incident during the battle, Corporal 'Friederich' Schiess of the NNC crept out from the biscuit-box wall, and leapt onto the abandoned barricade to bayonet and shoot Zulus crouching below. (Alan Perry)

and leaned across to fire down on the Zulus crouching on the other side. A Zulu snapped back at him with his musket, and although the bullet missed its mark, it blew Schiess' hat off. Schiess immediately jumped up, retrieved his hat and 'bayoneted the Zulu and shot a second, and bayoneted a third who came to their assistance, and then returned to his place'.

Despite such gallantry, pressure on the wall remained intense. Several times individual Zulus climbed right up onto the barricade before being driven back. Private Hitch saw a Zulu about to stab Bromhead. He presented his rifle at him, knowing it to be unloaded, and the Zulu dropped back out of the way. A few minutes later Hitch himself was fully occupied fighting a man in front of him when he saw another nearby point his rifle at him. There was nothing he could do, and the bullet struck Hitch in the shoulder, knocking him down. The Zulu rushed up to finish him off, but Bromhead shot him with his revolver. Hitch's wound was a terrible one – his shoulder blade was shattered, and Surgeon Reynolds later extracted 39 pieces of bone from it – but Hitch must have been a tough man, for someone bound it up for him with the lining from a great-coat, and he thrust his arm through his waist-belt to support the dead weight. He swapped his rifle for Bromhead's revolver, and used it as long as he was able; then he handed out ammunition to his comrades until at last he passed out from loss of blood. He came to the next morning when the battle was over.

Despite such casualties, morale within the garrison remained high, if only because, as several of them admitted afterwards, their situation was so desperate that it was simply a case of 'do or die'. Chaplain Smith, a tall red-bearded man who wore a faded black overcoat, passed along the line, handing out ammunition and cheering the men on, sternly rebuking any obscenities that caught his ear. 'Don't swear boys,' he is said to have exhorted them, 'and shoot them.' Around nightfall a rumour passed round that British troops could be seen on the Helpmekaar road. It was encouraging news, and the men let out a cheer which caused the Zulus to pause in their attacks for a few minutes. Chard admitted that he saw nothing himself, but the rumour undoubtedly helped to stiffen the defenders' resolve. Curiously enough, the two companies of the 24th at Helpmekaar did move down from the heights at about this time, accompanied by Major Spalding. They met a stream of refugees from Isandlwana, however, who declared that the post had fallen, a view which seemed to be confirmed by the distant smudge of smoke hanging over Shiyane. At the bottom of the heights scouts ran into a line of Zulus – presumably some of those who had broken away to pillage the area – who rapidly deployed across the road, and Spalding decided to return to Helpmekaar, to make a stand there.

By about 7.00pm, Chard's position had been reduced to the storehouse, a few square yards of ground in front of it, and the cattle-kraal. Several times the Zulus had run straight up to the back of the building, but there was no way for them to get in, and they had been driven back by fire from the loopholes and the men posted in the attic. As they had done so successfully at the hospital, the Zulus tried repeatedly to set fire to the roof, tossing into the thatch spears tied with bundles of blazing grass. Unable to remain close to the walls, however, they did not succeed; one man was actually shot just as he applied the light to the roof.

Sergeant Henry Gallagher of B Company, 2nd/24th, photographed in the early 1880s. Gallagher was apparently in charge of the back barricade during the early part of the fight, and was later stationed in the mealie-bag redoubt; he received a powder-burn on his right cheek from his Martini-Henry rifle, and carried this reminder of the battle for the rest of his life. (Major E.H. Lane)

Still piled up in front of the store were two tall pyramids of mealie-bags, which had not yet been used to form barricades. Assistant Commissary Dunne offered to form them into a redoubt; this was dangerous work, since they stood out above the height of the barricade, and were therefore exposed to Zulu fire. Dunne was a tall man, and as he stood on the heaps the bullets whistled and whined around him, but he was not hit. He dragged the bags together to form a single heap, hollowing out the summit so as to provide a bastion large enough to contain the worst of the wounded and a handful of riflemen. Because of their elevated position, these men could fire over the heads of the men on the main barricades, and add their fire against any fresh attack as it developed.

THE FIGHTING AFTER DARK

Under normal circumstances, it was not Zulu practice to fight during the night. Dependant as they were on hand-to-hand fighting, it was usually too difficult for them to co-ordinate their attacks after dark, and the night was, in any case, a time of ill omen, when the dark spiritual forces that might bring disaster lingered much closer to the surface of the everyday world. Nevertheless, when the sun went down, at about 7.30pm on the evening of 22 January, the Zulu attacks continued unabated. It is not hard to see

Darkness brought no let-up in the ferocity of the Zulu attacks, but as this contemporary engraving suggests, the flames from the burning hospital at least provided enough light for the defenders to fire by.
(Rai England collection)

61

Much of the battle of Rorke's Drift took place after dark, when the battle was lit by the flames from the burning hospital (right). The Zulus concentrated in the shadows, making the most of natural cover, and mounted a series of fierce assaults on the cattle kraal (left). Though they were able to force the British out of the kraal, they could not

penetrate Chard's final bastion, the storehouse and the small patch of ground in front of it. The mealie-bag redoubt gave the British an extra line of fire, which they could concentrate against each fresh attack. (Alan Perry)

LEFT *After dark, the fiercest Zulu attacks were directed against the cattle-kraal, the furthest point from the blazing hospital (where Witt's house stands, background). (Author's photo)*

BELOW *The cattle-kraal was a well-built structure affording good cover to the defenders, but the Zulu assaults were so tenacious that the British were driven back first to the interior partition, then to the near wall. This kraal has been reconstructed on the spot where it stood during the battle. (Author's photo)*

Zulus loom up out of the smoke and darkness to assault Chard's final position in one of the many attacks that took place after nightfall. (Author's collection)

why. It must have seemed to them that they were very close indeed to victory. The British had been driven out of the hospital, which was now on fire, and the enemy held only a small piece of ground. It was difficult to assess the extent of British casualties from outside the walls, but the Zulus themselves were suffering heavily, and it was surely likely that the British were now also in a bad way. To the warriors in the long grass, among the bush at the front of the post or lying around the scattered out-buildings, it must have seemed that one last effort would win the day.

Yet luck was against them. By now the damp roof of the hospital had long since caught fully alight, sending a tall plume of flames and sparks up into the sky. The fire cast a pool of light perhaps 40 or 50 yards around the building, lighting up the western end of the battlefield as bright as day. Although the Zulus could still mass safely out in the darkness, they could not reach the barricades without crossing this exposed area, and as they did so the British poured a tremendous volume of fire into them. 'Before they had time to retreat,' recalled Trooper Lugg of the Natal Mounted Police, 'we poured bullets into them like hail. We could see them falling in scores.' Unable to withstand this concentrated fire, the Zulus fell back into the shadows. Frustrated at the front of the post, they turned their attentions instead to the far eastern end of the perimeter Here they could approach the cattle-kraal without having to cross ground illuminated by the glare from the hospital.

The kraal consisted of drystone walling piled up to shoulder height. There was an interior partition across the middle and an opening on the storehouse side, so that while the defenders could move through it easily, the Zulus were faced with an uninterrupted wall. Nevertheless, in a series of vicious attacks, launched at very close range, they succeeded in driving the defenders back from the far wall, first to the interior partition, and then, abandoning the kraal completely, to the near wall. Some fragments of the story of this fight survive. Private Minehan of the 24th was fighting at the barricade when he felt a tug on his leg. He looked down to see a black hand emerging from the piles of straw. A Zulu had slipped into the kraal and crawled unnoticed through it, but before he could drag Minehan down, Minehan ran him through with the bayonet, skewering him to the ground. The Zulus did not achieve anything by driving out the defenders; the men in the redoubt could fire right down into their position, and every time a warrior showed his head, the soldiers on the near wall fired at him at a range so close that they could almost touch him with the muzzles of their rifles.

Once the attack on the cattle-kraal had produced a stalemate, the fighting began to die down. The garrison could hear the Zulu izinduna shouting commands out in the darkness, and every now and then a shout of 'Usuthu!', and a rattle of spears on shields would herald a fresh attack. Yet the Zulus were clearly tiring, and with each charge that was repulsed their hope of success diminished.

The last charge was made sometime between 9.00pm and 10.00pm, and its defeat was greeted by an exhausted British cheer; as one Zulu wryly put it later, by this time 'it was no longer fighting; they were exchanging salutations merely'.

Chard's men were also exhausted, and in addition to the seriously wounded, most of them had suffered cuts and knocks, or had burned their fingers on the barrels of their rifles, which had grown almost red-hot with the constant firing. Many had badly bruised shoulders from the heavy recoil of their rifles; when it became too painful to fire from the right shoulder, they had swapped arms, until their left shoulders also became bruised. Finally they had simply rested their rifles on the barricade, held them at arm's length, and fired away, hoping to discourage the Zulus by the volume of their fire rather than the accuracy. Loss of blood, adrenalin, and the sheer emotional ordeal of the struggle had left the men desperately thirsty. Their water-bottles must have been running low, for some time after the last attack Bromhead, Hook and a few others risked the Zulu fire to run out into the yard and haul back the water-cart which had been abandoned there. They ran the leather hose across the biscuit-box wall to slake the men's thirst.

The Zulu fire continued intensely until after midnight. Then it died away, only to splutter into life again several times. Confused shouts echoed around the post, and Chard and Bromhead climbed onto the mealie-bag redoubt and peered out into the blackness in an anxious attempt to see if new attacks were being mustered. Yet none came, and the last shots were fired at 4.00am on 23 January, shortly before dawn.

THE MORNING AFTER

The scene around Rorke's Drift at the first grey light was one of utter devastation. The roof of the hospital had fallen in, but here and there the thatch still smouldered, and a dense pall of smoke hung over the battlefield. It carried with it the stench of burnt flesh, from the remains of those who had died inside its walls and been cremated. The yard was littered with discarded and torn uniforms, battered helmets, shields and spears, and carpeted with cartridge cases and the brown paper packages with which they had been supplied. Chard's men had started the battle with a full com-

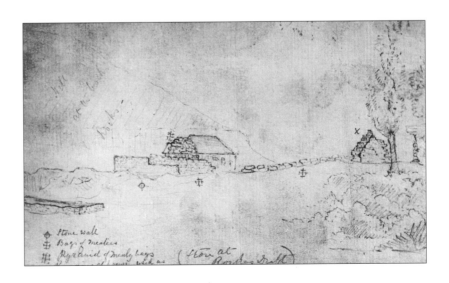

LEFT *The Morning after. Chard, Bromhead and the exhausted garrison search for signs of relief, surrounded by heaps of Zulu dead. (Author's collection)*

RIGHT *Surgeon Reynolds continued to tend the wounded throughout the fight, at great personal risk to himself, and was subsequently awarded the VC. (Author's collection)*

OVERLEAF *Aftermath: dawn on 23 January revealed to the battered and exhausted defenders the terrible price the Zulus had paid for their tenacity. The area in front of the gutted hospital, in particular, was carpeted with their dead, where the fighting had raged backwards and forwards across a few square yards of ground. At Rorke's Drift, both sides were fought to a standstill; on the morning of the 23rd, Chard's men were in no position to sustain a further serious attack, but nor were the Zulus able to mount one. (Michael Perry)*

pany reserve supply of ammunition, around 20,000 rounds; as Chard admitted, by the morning they had only a box and a half – about 900 rounds – left.

The post resembled an abattoir, with corpses piled up in grotesque positions all around the barricades. In front of the hospital, where the Zulus had charged back and forth across the veranda several times, the bodies were piled up on one another three deep in places, their limbs grotesquely twisted around one another, dead hands reaching out imploringly from the tangle. Below the ledge and against the barricade they were also heaped up, and in one place one tall warrior was found upside down, his heels on the top of the barricade, his head on the ground, and his body supported by the corpses of his comrades. Chard noted some of the curious wounds – one man's head spilt in half as if with an axe, and another with just a

Lieutenant Chard's revolver; believed to be the one he used during the fight. Chard is also known to have armed himself with a Martini-Henry on occasion throughout the battle. (Royal Engineers Museum, Chatham)

Chard's water-bottle; an unusual pattern – presumably a private purchase – rather than the issue 'Oliver' type. (Royal Engineers Museum, Chatham)

small mark where a bullet had struck him between the eyes, but with the back of his head blown away. A number of corpses were found in a similar position, crouched forward with their knees drawn up, their chins almost resting on their knees; no doubt something in the velocity of the Martini-Henry bullet had caused them to double up in this way. Presumably many of these Zulus were still alive, though badly wounded, but Surgeon Reynolds was fully occupied with the British casualties, even had he wanted to succour the enemy.

One brave Zulu had spent the night crouching uninjured in the cattle-kraal, and he suddenly stood up, fired at the astonished garrison, missed, and turned away towards the river; although shots were fired after him, Chard was rather pleased to see that 'the plucky fellow got off'.

Here and there were British dead; one or two had been repeatedly stabbed and disembowelled according to Zulu custom, but Private Hook recalled that he saw one man apparently still leaning against the barricade, defending his post. Hook spoke to him, but the man made no reply; when

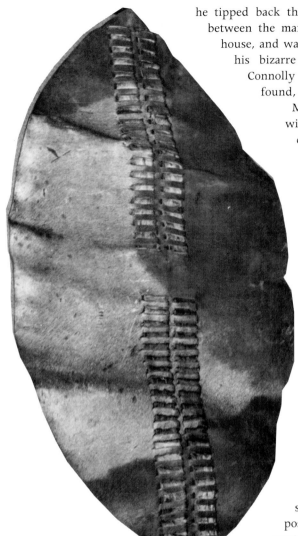

A red shield with white patches – said to be the colours of the uDloko ibutho – recovered from the battlefield at Rorke's Drift, and bearing a bullet-hole in the centre. (RRW Museum, Brecon)

he tipped back the man's helmet, Hook saw the mark of a bullet between the man's eyes. Private Waters rose up from the cook-house, and was almost shot by one of the garrison, who mistook his bizarre appearance for that of a Zulu. Howard and Connolly emerged from the bush, and poor Beckett was found, still alive, but dying.

Most importantly, however, the Zulus seemed to have withdrawn. Chard's garrison was exhausted, physically and emotionally spent, but the possibility of a new attack remained very real, and the officers could not afford to let them rest. Men were sent up on to the roof of the storehouse, to pull down the thatch, while others attached ropes to the walls of the hospital and pulled them down where they could, to prevent the Zulus using them as cover. The battered mealie-bags were hauled back into position, and the barricades were strengthened. Patrols were sent out to collect in the Zulu weapons. Hook had wandered some way off, with a bundle of spears over his shoulder and his rifle in the other hand, when he saw a man bleeding profusely from the leg. No doubt his senses were dulled by the fight, for he walked on until the man suddenly made a grab for his rifle, seizing the butt. Hook dropped the spears and managed to cling onto the muzzle, and for a few moments the two pulled back and forth, until at last Hook pulled the rifle free, struck the Zulu in the chest, then finished him off.

Then, about 7.00am, a body of Zulus came into sight once more from behind Shiyane, and took up a position on KwaSingqindi hill, opposite to the south-west. Chard immediately called his patrols in, and the garrison took up their posts. It was an anxious moment, for the defenders were clearly in no position to withstand a further determined assault. The Zulus made no move to advance, however, but squatted silently out of rifle range, until at last, to the garrison's relief, they rose up and returned the way they had come.

THE ZULU WITHDRAWAL AND LORD CHELMSFORD'S MOVEMENTS

The Zulu withdrawal had probably begun shortly after the last failed attacks, at around 10.00pm the night before. The effort required to assault the post with such tenacity for six hours had been extraordinary. Moreover, the warriors had begun the battle only after crossing 12 or 15 miles of rugged terrain on their advance from the bivouac before Isandlwana to the river. They had probably not eaten since mid-morning,

THE ZULU WITHDRAWAL AND CHELMSFORD'S RETURN

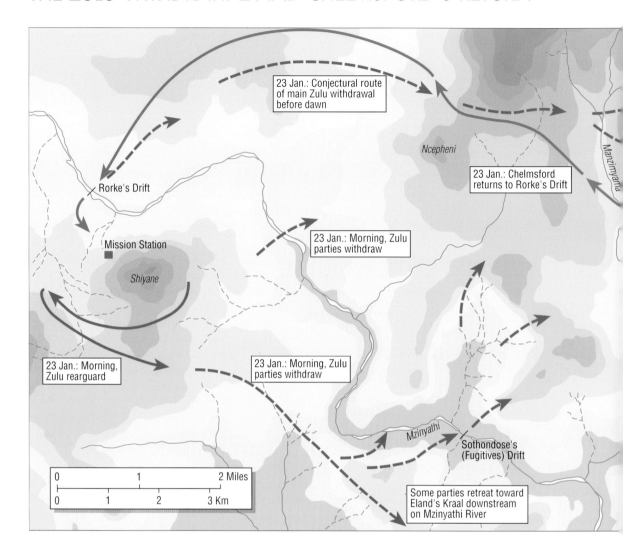

23 Jan.: Conjectural route of main Zulu withdrawal before dawn

Ncepheni

23 Jan.: Chelmsford returns to Rorke's Drift

Manzinyama

Rorke's Drift

Mission Station

Shiyane

23 Jan.: Morning, Zulu parties withdraw

23 Jan.: Morning, Zulu rearguard

23 Jan.: Morning, Zulu parties withdraw

Mzinyathi

Sothondose's (Fugitives) Drift

Some parties retreat toward Eland's Kraal downstream on Mzinyathi River

| 0 | 1 | 2 Miles |
| 0 | 1 | 2 | 3 Km |

and throughout the fight their nearest water supply was the Mzinyathi river, half a mile away. Nevertheless, they had repeatedly attacked the post in the face of a withering fire, and had been engaged in prolonged bouts of hand-to-hand combat. Some inkling of the exhaustion this produced can be gleaned from the story of a party of Natal traders who found themselves near Eland's Kraal, some miles downstream from Rorke's Drift, on the morning of 23 January. They reported that they had been approached by groups of warriors making their way home, who were so tired that they were dragging their shields after them. The Zulus had greeted the traders politely and walked on.

Furthermore, the attacks had been desperately costly. According to Chard, 351 Zulu bodies were dragged away from the barricades immediately after the fight and buried in two large pits at the front of the post.

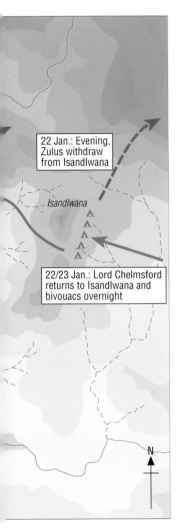

22 Jan.: Evening, Zulus withdraw from Isandlwana

Isandlwana

22/23 Jan.: Lord Chelmsford returns to Isandlwana and bivouacs overnight

N

He admitted, however, that this was not a true reflection of their losses, since bodies turned up for days, and even weeks, afterwards. Many lay out on the line of retreat, and a pile of bloodied shields on the banks of the river near the Drift indicated that friends and relatives of the wounded had been able to drag them at least that far. But the river was high, and many no doubt could not be helped safely across; furthermore, a number of the dead were probably tipped into the waters. Others turned up in the caves on Shiyane, where some had fallen in the fight or been dragged into crevices and covered over in simple burial. One source, quoting information gleaned from the Zulus themselves, suggested that as many as 600 had been killed altogether. On top of this, an unknown number had been wounded, some of them more than once. Years later Trooper Lugg met a Zulu who had been hit no less than four times at Rorke's Drift and survived. The close quarters in which the fighting took place and the shock caused by Martini-Henry wounds at such a range probably resulted in a higher proportion of killed to wounded than was usual in battle, but even allowing that 300 or 400 men might have been wounded, the total number of Zulu casualties might have been close to 1,000. In other words, as many as one in four of the attackers suffered some sort of injury, a quite extraordinary number, which speaks volumes for their courage and persistence.

Clearly it would have required superhuman effort to continue the assault indefinitely under such circumstances, and by 10.00pm it must have been obvious that not only were the British unlikely to be overrun, they were as secure as ever behind their barricades. No doubt some warriors slipped away then, of their own accord; parties were later seen crossing back into Zululand at various points along the Mzinyathi, as far downstream as Sothondose's Drift. The main body probably left in good order some time after midnight, and seems to have crossed at Rorke's Drift. Quite who the party were that Chard saw on the morning of 23 January remains uncertain, but they had all the appearance of an organised rearguard.

Along the line of retreat, the main Zulu body passed close to Lord Chelmsford's men, moving in the opposite direction. Chelmsford had spent much of the previous day in the Mangeni hills, about 12 miles from Isandlwana. He had not found the main Zulu army he sought, but did encounter small parties of warriors, with whom he skirmished throughout the day. When the first reports of an attack on the camp reached him, he was not particularly alarmed, and it was some time before he was convinced of the seriousness of the situation. By the time he had marched his men back to Isandlwana, it was evening, and all that remained of the Zulu army was a line of stragglers disappearing over the hills in the distance. Even then, the true magnitude of the disaster seemed incomprehensible, and Chelmsford's command clung to the belief that some part of the camp's garrison must have fallen back on Rorke's Drift. Cut off in enemy territory, unaware of the true extent of the defeat and concerned at the whereabouts of the Zulu army, Chelmsford had little choice but to bivouac on the battlefield, and his men passed a terrible night amid the ruins of battle. They stumbled over bodies in the darkness, and in some cases awoke next morning to find they had been sleeping next to the corpses of men they knew. In the distance the fire from the burning hospital at Rorke's Drift offered the grim possibility that the Zulus had crossed into Natal behind them.

Chelmsford roused his command before dawn on 23 January, and set them marching back towards Rorke's Drift. A few miles from Isandlwana they were greeted with the extraordinary spectacle of the Zulu force retreating from the Drift. Chelmsford's men were exhausted, and had only the ammunition each soldier carried with him, and the general was reluctant to initiate a full-scale battle. However, the Zulus were in no condition to fight, and their column crossed his front, moving into the hills behind Isandlwana. At times the two forces were within a few hundred yards of each other, and some of Chelmsford's black auxiliaries called across conversationally to the Zulus. Apart from a few shots fired by stragglers, neither side showed any interest in launching an attack.

ABOVE *Private William Roy, 24th Regiment, a patient in the hospital who earned the DCM for his part in its defence. (Author's collection)*

LEFT *Corporal F. Attwood of the Army Service Corps, who received the DCM for his actions at Rorke's Drift. (RLC Museum)*

RIGHT *Wheeler J. Cantwell RA, who was also awarded the DCM. (Royal Archives)*

THE RELIEF

By about 7.00am Chelmsford's men had reached the river. Everything they had seen so far had led them to believe that the post had fallen. Chelmsford carefully deployed some of his men to cover the crossing, and sent his mounted infantry ahead to scout out the post. This was also a tense moment for Chard and his men; Chelmsford had a regiment of the Natal Native Contingent with him, and from a distance it seemed to the garrison that his force was the main Zulu army, come from Isandlwana to finish them off. But the truth was revealed as the mounted men galloped up, and Chard's men greeted their relief by climbing on to the barricades, cheering and throwing their hats into the air.

Nevertheless, it was a time of mixed emotions for Chelmsford's command. It soon became clear that none of the force left behind at Isandlwana had managed to retire on the post, and that the disaster had been complete. Feelings were running high among his men, who had glimpsed some of the horrors in the fallen camp that night, and as the column came up, the Natal Native Contingent and some of the infantry were sent over the battlefield to flush out the wounded Zulus. Several dozen were found lying in the bush at the front of the post, and they were stabbed and clubbed to death so as not to waste ammunition.

In fact it is unlikely that the British could have done much for them, even had they been inclined. Chelmsford's command had taken little enough with it when it had advanced to Mangeni the morning before, and all of their tents, baggage, bedding and supplies had been lost with the camp. The bodies were dragged away and buried, and the barricades extended as the column prepared to spend the first of many uncomfortable nights around the post. Some of the colonial volunteers, who were told to sleep in the cattle-kraal, awoke the next morning to find that the straw on which they had been lying still concealed several dead Zulus.

The rain returned in torrents, and with nothing to shelter under, the entire command had to snatch what sleep they could lying out in the open

RIGHT *Private Fred Hitch of B Company, who was shot through the shoulder by a Zulu crouching below the rocky ledge. Hitch continued to fight on at the barricade while he was able, and then distributed ammunition to the defenders until too weak from loss of blood. His extraordinary courage earned him the VC. (Royal Archives)*

Relief: Chelmsford's mounted infantry ride up to the post on the morning of 23 January. (Nottingham Castle collection).

in the mud. B Company were at least accorded the place of honour, sleeping in the attic of the storehouse, where a tarpaulin had been stretched across the bare rafters. The stockpile of stores, which had proved so vital to their survival, provided ample provisions for those to whom hunger provided an antidote to squeamishness.

Chard had lost 15 men in the fight, and ten were badly wounded, two of them mortally; an astonishingly small number considering the intensity of the battle. The dead were buried at the back of the post, and a stone memorial was later erected on the spot. Most wounds had been in the upper part of the body and caused by rifle-fire rather than edged weapons, indicating the extent to which they had successfully kept the Zulus out of the reach of their stabbing spears. Over the next few days the wounded were evacuated to Helpmekaar, although conditions there were scarcely better. Inevitably, in the cramped and unsanitary conditions around the post, men began to fall ill, and over the next few weeks a number died, and were buried alongside the battlefield dead. Several of the defenders were also stricken, including Chard and Dunne, who were sent down to Ladysmith to recuperate.

AFTERMATH

Although the remainder of Chelmsford's old Centre Column spent several uncomfortable weeks cooped up at Rorke's Drift in nightly expectation of a fresh Zulu attack, no such attack ever came. To the British it seemed that the defence of Rorke's Drift had saved Natal from a Zulu invasion, but from the Zulu viewpoint, that had never been either practical or intended. Indeed, the terrible events of 22 January had proved as costly for the Zulus as they had for the British; even at a conservative estimate, Isandlwana and Rorke's Drift had cost the Zulus at least 1,500 dead and hundreds more wounded. It was a heavy blow for a citizen army like the Zulus to withstand, and border agents reported that the sound of mourning dirges could be heard along the Mzinyathi and the Thukela for weeks afterwards. So great was the shock that the army dispersed to recover, and the king was not able to muster it again before March. Not that King Cetshwayo had any more intention of invading in the aftermath of Isandlwana than he had had when the war had begun a fortnight before; he continued to insist on a defensive strategy, and in doing so he allowed the initiative to return to the British, with ultimately fatal results for his kingdom.

To the British, the victory at Rorke's Drift seemed all the more significant in the aftermath of the shock of Isandlwana, and the battle soon achieved a significance which far outweighed its true strategic importance. It proved that when the chips were down the ordinary British soldier could still be relied upon. The thin red line had held, and Tommy Atkins had done his duty. The garrison were hailed as heroes, not only in Natal, but across the Empire, and no fewer than 11 of them were awarded the Victoria Cross – including Chard, Bromhead, Dalton, Hook and Hitch – while a further five received the Silver Medal for Distinguished Conduct.

By comparison the Zulus returned home to the ridicule of their nation. In trying to capture some of the glory which had eluded them at Isandlwana, they had merely made themselves a laughing stock. As one Zulu put it, the uThulwana 'were finished up at Jim's, shocking coward's they were too. Our people laughed at them, some said "You! You're no men! You're just women, seeing that you ran away for no reason at all, like the wind!" Others jeered and said, "You marched off. You went to dig little bits with your assegais out of the house of Jim that had never done you

For the British the stand at Rorke's Drift was a moral triumph which helped to offset the disaster at Isandlwana. For the Zulus it was nothing more than a costly mopping-up side-show, the precursor of six months of bitter fighting which ultimately saw the destruction of their army – here at oNdini on 4 July – and the break-up of the kingdom. (Author's collection)

Chard was present at the final battle of the Anglo-Zulu War, at oNdini (Ulundi) on 4 July. This shield, which he took as a souvenir, bears the inscription 'From Ulundi 4th July 1879' and his signature. (Royal Engineers Museum, Chatham)

LEFT Chard was presented with his VC in the field by Sir Garnet Wolseley. (Author's collection)

any harm!"' Prince Dabulamanzi hedged his report of the battle, pointing out that he had successfully stormed the hospital, but in truth he had nothing to show for his disobedience, and he retired to his personal homestead under a cloud of royal disapproval. It was a harsh judgement on men who had fought every bit as courageously as the victors.

The tide of war soon moved on from Rorke's Drift. The defeat at Isandlwana had shattered Chelmsford's original invasion plan, but the reinforcements denied him before the war were now made good in abundance. Cetshwayo's magnanimity allowed him time to reorganise and mount a fresh invasion. In a second wave of fighting, at the end of March, the Zulus were heavily defeated, and by the beginning of July Chelmsford had pushed a column to the very doorstep of oNdini. The last great battle was fought on 4 July, and the Zulus were defeated. Chelmsford returned to Britain a hero, and British troops withdrew from Zululand. King Cetshwayo was captured and sent into exile, and the Anglo-Zulu War was over.

THE BATTLEFIELD TODAY

The Reverend Otto Witt returned to his mission when hostilities ended. Nothing remained of his house, and the British had converted the store into a stone-walled fort. Witt rebuilt his house on the foundations of the old hospital, and knocked down the store, replacing it with a neat church. Although they post-date the battle, it is these historic buildings which mark the site today.

Rorke's Drift is one of the best-known battlefields in South Africa, but despite a steady trickle of tourists, it still has something of the air of a frontier mission. The nearest town, Dundee, is over 50 kilometres away; anyone visiting the sight can either approach it from that direction or, if they are more adventurous, follow Chelmsford's old line of communication, along the road which runs from Pietermaritzburg, through Greytown and on to Helpmekaar via the spectacular Thukela valley. Helpmekaar consists of little more than a police-station and a store, hardly more than it did in 1879, but the road still drops down off the heights towards Rorke's Drift.

There is accommodation available in Dundee, or on a number of farms nearer the battlefield, but it is always best to arrange this in advance. Rorke's old farm is still owned by the Evangelical Lutheran Church, and although it boasts no village, it is home to over 2,000 people, whose houses, stores and schools are scattered across the area at the foot of Shiyane. Until recently there was little to mark the site of the battle itself, although the spot remains easily recognisable from contemporary illustrations. Today, however, an excellent museum is contained in Witt's old house, and includes life-sized figurines, moving-light displays, commentaries, dioramas and a few relics of the battle. The building itself is very similar to the old hospital, apart from a tin roof in place of the thatch, and it requires very little imagination to conjure up the events which took place there during the battle.

Outside, the lines of the barricades were first traced earlier this century by a local resident who placed stones in the grass. More recent archaeological investigation, which confirmed the location of the store's foundations, suggested that they were slightly misaligned, and they have recently been adjusted. The cattle-kraal has been rebuilt on the spot where it stood during the battle. A leaflet is available in the museum which enables the visitor to wander the site and identify the features. Visitors are

The Rorke's Drift Museum today includes life-sized displays representing a section of the barricade. (Author's photo)

often surprised to see just how small the British perimeter was, especially after the retreat to the storehouse: it takes just a few paces to walk across it.

On the whole, the vegetation has increased significantly in the area since the time of the battle. A line of trees was planted in the walled enclosure, marking the British graves, while several small buildings and patches of bush obscure the view to the Shiyane terraces. Nevertheless, it is still possible to walk up to the terraces, and the caves and boulders have changed very little since the Zulu marksmen occupied them. Nearby, bored members of Chelmsford's force carved their numbers into the sandstone in the weeks after the battle, while a mission bell stands on the terrace above the point from which local legend suggests that Prince Dabulamanzi directed the fight. The very energetic would find it worthwhile to walk up the steep shoulder of the hill, and press on to the summit. From here there is a splendid view of the Mzinyathi, stretching from beyond Rorke's Drift upstream on the left to Sothondose's Drift – now called Fugitives' Drift – on the right. This is the view which greeted Witt, Reynolds and Chaplain Smith on the morning of the battle. The distinctive crag of Isandlwana – itself one of the most affecting battlefields in the world – is clearly visible opposite.

A monument marks the site of the British dead, between the old post and the Shiyane terraces, but the location of the Zulus' graves is not quite so certain. Monuments were erected to them in front of the post and at the foot of the hill in 1979, and an older site, surrounded by a stone wall and marked by several stone 'heads of grief' lies to the south, behind some school buildings.

The battlefield is well looked after, and on the whole has a peaceful and pleasant atmosphere. For those staying nearby, it is worth lingering till dusk, for it is at this time of day, when the battle itself was raging, that the site is most atmospheric.

CHRONOLOGY

Note: the exact timing of some events during the battle is uncertain, since the accounts of the various participants – who were, after all, preoccupied – do not always tally. The following chronology is therefore no more than approximate; where there is considerable conflict, timings are taken from Chard's accounts, which seem to be the most reliable.

22/23 JANUARY 1879

12.30–2.30pm – Sound of distant firing from Isandlwana heard at Rorke's Drift. Black troops, thought to be NNC, seen approaching Mzinyathi river in the direction of Sothondose's Drift.

3.15-3.30pm – First survivors from Isandlwana arrive at both the post and Chard's camp at the Drift. Chard returns to post; garrison begin building barricades.

3.45pm – Party of approx. 100 men of the Natal Native Horse arrive at the post from the Drift, and deploy behind Shiyane hill to delay Zulu advance.

4.20pm – First shots of the battle; the Natal Native Horse break before the oncoming Zulus, and flee in the direction of Helpmekaar. The NNC stationed at the post are unnerved by the sight, and also flee.

4.30pm – The first Zulus come into sight; 600 men of the iNdluyengwe attack the back of the post but are checked, and veer round to occupy the bush at the front of the post. The first attacks on the front of the hospital begin.

4.50pm – The main Zulu force arrives, and advances to occupy the bush at the front of the post. Zulu riflemen also occupy the Shiyane terrace. The battle begins in earnest with severe attacks on the front of the hospital, and a galling fire from the hill at the rear.

RIGHT *Fort Bromhead – built around the old storehouse – looking towards KwaSingqindi hill (left background), where the Zulus reappeared on the morning of 23 January. (Author's collection)*

6.30pm – The casualties from the fire on Shiyane being too heavy to bear, Chard orders his men to abandon the yard and retire to the biscuit-box wall. Attacks on the front of the post continue.

6.00–7.30pm – The fight for the hospital; the Zulus succeed in setting fire to the roof.

7.00pm – Sunset.

7.00–8.00pm – Zulu attacks on the front of the post are thwarted by the light of the burning hospital.

8.00–9.00pm – Zulus repeatedly assault the eastern end of the post, and drive the defenders out of the cattle-kraal.

9.00–10.00pm – Last Zulu assaults; attacks are losing momentum.

10.00pm–2.00am – Fire-fight continues with some intensity throughout the night; Zulu withdrawal begins.

4.00am – Last shots fired by Zulus.

4.30am – Dawn; the Zulus have withdrawn. Chard sends out patrols to collect up Zulu weapons and strip thatch from storehouse roof.

7.00am – Significant body of Zulus appears to south-east of post on KwaSingqindi hill. After some minutes they retire in the direction of Sothondose's Drift.

8.00am – Arrival of Lord Chelmsford's column.

WARGAMING RORKE'S DRIFT

The opening engagements of the Zulu War differed as dramatically in their scale as in their results, the areas fought over contrasting even more strikingly than the numbers engaged. The British position at Rorke's Drift was only 100 metres long, and about 50 across, whereas the initial British deployment at Isandlwana spread over an area about two kilometres by three. If one looks at Chelmsford's operations of 21st-22nd January as a whole, then yet another change in perspective is required as these occurred over an area almost twenty kilometres square. These differences in scale show that wargaming the Zulu War can be approached in a variety of ways. Fortunately the underlying tactical considerations remain constant, although it may be necessary to play several types of game in order to appreciate the full flavour of the period.

Perhaps the most surprising aspect of these opening battles is the apparent contempt with which the British regarded their opponents. Examples of this abound, from Chelmsford's original decision to split his forces on 21 January to the failure to concentrate the defenders of the camp in a proper defensive perimeter. It is essential, if refighting Isandlwana, to disguise the scenario to prevent the British players taking undue advantage of hindsight. One approach might be to represent the game as a road building exercise, which in a sense it was, to be carried out in the face of an enemy well equipped with rifles. This would not only lead the British to over-extend by occupying the edge of the Nqutu plateau, but might even encourage them to fight in open order, as they had done successfully against the Xhosa. Only when the Zulu masses make their appearance should it become apparent that this might not be the best option.

Faced with greatly superior numbers of Zulus the British have difficult choices to make about how best to employ their superior weaponry. Troops in open order shoot better, as they aim more carefully and create less smoke, but the volume of fire may be insufficient to halt massed Zulus. Similarly, independent fire could be twice as lethal as volley fire, but uses up three times as much ammunition. Ammunition constraints are essential as these were a key factor in the collapse of British resistance at Isandlwana. If you don't like book-keeping, then an effective way of tracking ammunition expenditure is to issue every player with a handful of spent .22 cartridges which they have to give up in order to fire.

John Chard, looking suitably dashing on his return to Britain after the war. At the time of the battle, Chard was the senior officer present at Rorke's Drift, despite being only a lieutenant. On the day, he was probably bearded and wearing his undress uniform, rather than the full dress shown here. (Keith Reeves collection)

In the opening battles the few artillery weapons available to the British were largely ineffective. This was partly because the 7pdr. guns had too short a range (1500 metres approx.), and too low a muzzle velocity to fire shrapnel effectively. More seriously, they ran out of case shot, and tried to change position in front of the quicker moving Zulus. Similarly the rocket battery was overrun before coming into action. Artillery rules, therefore, should be very simple. Guns should be effective only in combination with infantry, increasing the moral, rather than the physical, effect of their fire.

To prevent games degenerating into endless bouts of hand-to-hand fighting, British fire should prevent Zulu movement, only inflicting losses if targets continue to move instead of taking cover. Zulu morale should be reduced for being under fire rather than by past losses. For example, they could dice in order to move, trying to score less than an initial morale value reduced by one for each company firing at them. An extra one could be deducted for artillery or volley fire.

Casualties could then be limited, while giving fire a direct influence on the course of the battle. Although Zulu casualties were higher, in percentage terms, at Isandlwana and Rorke's Drift than they would be later in the campaign, neither of the opening battles of 1879 saw any disastrous collapse of Zulu morale. When beaten off at Rorke's Drift, the Zulus fell back and took snuff. Had they been held at Isandlwana they might well have acted with similar insouciance. For the Zulus therefore these early battles should be ended by disorganisation and fatigue rather than flight, unless of course they win. These factors would relate more closely to the elapsed time from when they first go into action rather than the numbers of Zulus actually lost.

The rapidity with which the Zulus advanced, once committed, was a recognised problem for the British; orders were issued that Zulus should be regarded as cavalry. Over broken ground, however, they could often move faster than horsemen. Tactically this has two consequences for the British. Firstly, if they start the battle in the wrong place, it will be impossible to put this right in time, and secondly it is extremely helpful to have an obstacle to break the force of the Zulus' advance. This, of course, was the case at Rorke's Drift where the defenders exploited existing natural features, when they built their barricades. Attacking Zulus should fall back into cover if they fail to carry the barricades with their first rush, to try again later. On the other hand, when refighting Isandlwana, it is important, to prevent the British from forming a wagon laager. Zulu mobility also makes reconnaissance difficult for the British as their mounted scouts may be unable to get away once entangled in rough ground. This provides a role for the Natal Native Contingent, who could be counted on to move quickly over rough ground. However, their limited fighting ability provides little encouragement for the wargamer to place them in the front line as they were at Isandlwana. Perhaps the best approach is to force the British to hold a wide front, covering road-making, or escorting wagons, so they are forced to use the NNC, with possibly unfortunate results.

At Isandlwana the British forces could all be on the table as the Zulus knew where they were. Individual companies would hold on until their flanks were turned, or ammunition ran low, when they would try to fall back on the wagons. One way of representing the ill-coordinated British defence would be to move them exactly the distances rolled on their movement dice. This would make it difficult for them to form a coherent line, allowing the Zulus to infiltrate between them. The initial Imperial deployment could consist of cards placed face down around the camp in the historical position of individual companies. Some of these should be NNC, but which would only become apparent when the Zulus came into sight.

Much of the discussion so far has been from the British point of view. However, there is a strong case for recreating the Zulu War more directly from the Zulu standpoint. In general, colonial wargames work better viewed from the perspective of imperialism's victims. Too many wargamers begin by collecting a large, balanced force of imperial troops, without thinking about their more numerous opponents. At best this is wasteful as it is rarely possible to use all the troops produced in the original fit of enthusiasm. At worst it distorts the type of game played, as it becomes difficult to represent the native forces adequately. In reality, the typical colonial campaign saw scratch forces hastily collected to face some emergency, and the Zulu War was no exception. For the figure gamer therefore it makes more sense to begin by collecting as many Zulus as possible within the constraints of the available budget and playing space. When you have enough of them to form the four parts of the classic Zulu deployment, then is the time to consider how many British and Colonial troops are needed. As the numerical odds were generally heavily against them, relatively few Imperial figures should be necessary. Indeed a vital feature of any Zulu War refight should be the visual shock of the sheer quantity of Zulus. If you can't face painting them, it is possible to adopt various subterfuges to reduce the terrifyingly large numbers required. For example, much of the time many of them would be concealed, allowing figures to be reused. Alternatively, different figure scales can be used for the two sides.

In general however, the Zulus deserve better than to be treated as an afterthought. As regards mobility, discipline and courage the Zulu army was an almost perfect creation, its only deficiencies being in fire power and perhaps initiative. Unlike many of the Victorian Army's opponents, the Zulus had a well thought out set of battle tactics. These were applied by highly experienced leaders who remained apart from the tactical hurly-burly to direct operations in a manner readily appreciated today. It is well worth constructing a Zulu wargame, and not just another triumph for British arms. This might allow players to pin the enemy with the bull's Chest, or else lure them into difficult ground. Meanwhile the Horns would be turning the enemy's flanks, the Loins remaining under cover to deal the final blow. If individual players took separate wings of the Zulu army they could quite properly compete among themselves to kill more of their opponents, and gain more of the glory. Faced with British firepower, the Zulus need to take full advantage of concealment in order to bring their forces to close quarters before coming under fire. Deliberate displays of force by one wing could be used to distract attention from the decisive attack, approaching under cover from another direction.

However, that said, it must be recognised that part of the appeal of wargaming Rorke's Drift is to place the player quaking uncertainly in the shoes of the British garrison. Although some parts of the action lend themselves to small skirmish games – the fight for the hospital, for example, with the British player's victory conditions dependent upon evacuating as many of his figures as possible through the appropriate wall – it is undoubtedly satisfying to recreate the engagement as a whole. This is not impossible, especially on a club level; at the time of writing Redoubt Miniatures produce and excellent 25mm model of the buildings and barricades, complete with lift-off roofs and internal walls, which makes it much easier to duplicate the essential terrain features. In such a game the British garrison should be represented man for man – a total of roughly 150 figures, and you can name them individually if you want to! There are obvious problems with duplicating the Zulu strength, but there are ways to deal with this, which also avoid some of the pitfalls of the game.

Firstly, the playing area should consist of just the area around the buildings, with perhaps 20 (scale) metres of the surrounding area, with more included at the back than at the front. The terrain need only be flat, but to achieve the correct feel two thirds of the area should be raised up (polystyrene tiles?), with a step running across the front of the post, to represent the height advantage of the rocky ledge. The British player may begin the game with his barricades built – inadequately, in front of the hospital – and his men deployed to defend them. Now, one of the usual faults in playing the entire battle is that the Zulu player, aware of the problems which faced his historical counterpart, can simply attack one section of the line, braving initial casualties from British fire, and driving a wedge through the barricade. That done, it's very difficult to prevent him winning. However, in fact it was very difficult for the real Zulu commander to co-ordinate his forces fully, and to represent this, the Zulu player should only be allowed to bring his forces on piecemeal. Indeed, it should be assumed that the Zulus can gradually extend their position round the post off-table; what happens on the board, therefore, is simply the closequarter fighting, a succession of rushes to contact, represented in their final moments. Thus the Zulu player might be allowed initially to place as many as forty figures on the edge of the board facing the back of the post, to represent the initial rush. These have to run the gauntlet of British fire along the back wall, and their charge will probably fail to strike home; although some will survive, sheltered behind the cover of the cook-house and ovens, and able to fire at the defenders with firearms if they have them, the Zulu player will not be allowed to introduce more warriors from that direction to reinforce them. Instead, at intervals of a few moves, he will be allowed to bring figures on – in groups of no more than ten or 20 – on various narrow fronts around the edges of the table, working towards the front. This represents the Zulu encircling movement off-table, with the charges merely the tip of the iceberg; the Zulu player will constantly be trying to maintain impetus to make them strike home before they are disrupted, whilst the British player will be trying to concentrate his firepower against him. In places where there are insufficient redcoats to keep the Zulus back, such as round the hospital, the Zulu player will have the opportunity to move his men to contact, fight hand to hand, set fire to the roof, and so on. The rocky ledge should count as a serious obstacle, with the Zulus required to spend at least one turn clambering up it, before they can fight hand to hand; this allows the British player a chance to fire into them at point-black range, thereby duplicating the terrible 'killing zone' the ledge created. Once casualties mount up, the Zulu player will be required to choose whether he should allow the survivors of each individual rush to continue in suicidal charges, or hold them back, take advantage of what cover they can, and try to join up with subsequent fresh arrivals.

Once the Zulu player has worked round the entire front of the board, he should be allowed to bring his figures on anywhere he chooses, to keep the British guessing, but at the same time the frequency with which he can do so must be reduced, to represent flagging morale; it could even be decided by the turn of a card or the roll of a dice, to introduce an unpredictable element. Thus the Zulu player might find himself with an excellent tactical opportunity, but with insufficient troops on table to exploit it, and be thwarted by a bad roll of the dice which prevents him bringing on more in time! From a practical point of view, the staggered phases of fighting should reduce the number of Zulu figures in play at any given time, and allow for a certain amount of re-cycling. The fire from Zulus off-table should not be ignored, however, and some system should be devised of causing casualties amongst the British at random, perhaps by throwing a dice for one man each turn. The chances of him being killed or wounded should be higher if he is in the yard or on the front barricade, to represent fire from Shiyane; if the British player should fall back to the position in front of the storehouse, as happened in the real fight, the risk from such fire should be minimal, but not entirely overlooked. The British player might therefore suddenly loose Chard, Bromhead, or a man in a key sector of the line quite unexpectedly, allowing the Zulu player an opening. Although generally morale should not be a major factor in a game such as this — the British don't have much option but to fight, whilst to some extent it is already built in to the Zulu scenario — the presence of a senior British figure should have some positive effect on the performance of all British figures within a few yards of him, whilst conversely the death or injury of such a figure should have a temporary negative effect, to duplicate the effects of shock and dismay on those nearby. Victory conditions for each side are simple enough; the Zulus have to over-run the post and kill the defenders, whilst the garrison must just survive. The exhaustion which ultimately caused the Zulus to withdraw can be represented easily by giving the Zulu player a finite number of figures; once all have been introduced onto the board, it can be assumed that the rest, lying off-table, have abandoned hope of victory and will not commit themselves and the British have therefore won.

For games set in the open, British movement die rolls can be used to set off Zulu contacts, or again cards can be drawn for each fresh area of terrain entered, or passed. As Zulus can only be spotted at close range, the British must use their NNC and Colonial horse to scout ahead, or risk the main column being overrun before it can form a firing line. Once contact has been made, the Chest and perhaps one of the Horns are put into position, leaving open the possibility of a flank attack by the remaining Horn. The Loins should remain out of sight ready to replace one of the other units, if it falters. A British solo game is particularly suited to an operational level game ranging over the whole area covered by Chelmsford's reconnaissance of 21st-22nd January. There is no good reason why the Zulu army should not have attacked the mobile part of his column, rather than the camp at Isandlwana.

If the British fail to drive off their opponents, then it is open to the players to go down fighting or face the perils of Fugitive's Drift. Each player would take one figure, dicing for the quality of horse available, if any. They then have to follow the winding trail back to the comparative safety of Rorke's Drift, across swamps, chasms, and rocky torrents, at the mercy of Zulus deliberately sent ahead to cut off survivors. Horses become lame, revolvers jam, and friends who twist their ankles, must be rescued. The only hope will be that you put on your blue patrol jacket this morning, as the Zulus were entirely literal in their interpretation of the king's orders to kill the redcoats.

A GUIDE TO
FURTHER READING

Bennett, I., *Eyewitness in Zululand,* London, 1989. An important study of the role of the Commissaries in South Africa 1877-81, based on Walter Dunne's reminiscences.

Emery, F., *The Red Soldier,* London, 1979. Eyewitness accounts of the war from the British perspective, including a good chapter on Rorke's Drift.

Holme, N., *The Silver Wreath,* London, 1979. A list of the men of the 24th who fought at Isandlwana and Rorke's Drift, including a detailed analysis of the Rorke's Drift rolls, which also includes a number of British accounts of the battle.

Knight, I., *Zulu War 1879; Twilight of a Warrior Nation,* Osprey Campaign series No. 14. A detailed and extensively illustrated account of the entire 1879 campaign.

Knight, I., *Nothing Remains But To Fight; The Defence of Rorke's Drift,* London, 1993. A comprehensive study of the battle, based entirely on contemporary accounts, with many illustrations.

Knight, I., *Zulu; The Battles of Rorke's Drift and Isandlwana,* London, 1992. An exhaustive study of the Isandlwana campaign.

Knight, I., *Brave Men's Blood,* London, 1990. A pictorial history of the war as a whole.

Knight, I. and Castle, I., *The Zulu War; Then and Now,* London, 1993. A comparative study of the battlefields as they were in 1879 and are today.

Knight, I. and Scollins, R., *British Forces in Zululand 1879,* Osprey Elite series No. 32. A detailed study of the British organisation and uniforms of the war. Includes 12 plates of original colour artwork

Knight, I. and McBride, A., *The Zulus,* Osprey Elite series No. 21. A detailed analysis of the organisation and costume of the Zulu army. Includes 12 plates of original colour artwork

Laband, J. and Thompson, P., *Kingdom and Colony at War, Pietermaritzburg and Cape Town,* 1990. A series of essays on various aspects of the Anglo-Zulu War, including the NNC and Zulu at Rorke's Drift.

Laband, J. and Thompson, P., *The Buffalo Border, Durban, 1983.* A study of the Rorke's Drift area throughout the campaign.

Laband, J., *Kingdom In Crisis; The Zulu Response To The British Invasion of 1879,* Manchester, 1992. A definitive account of the war from the Zulu perspective.

INDEX

(References to illustrations are shown in **bold**)

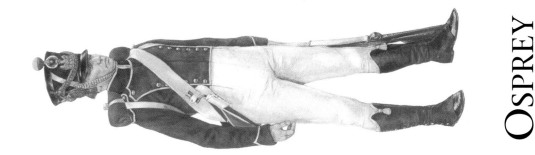

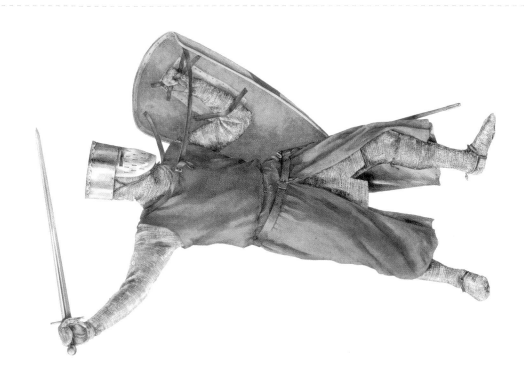

FIND OUT MORE ABOUT OSPREY

❑ Please send me the latest listing of Osprey's publications

❑ I would like to subscribe to Osprey's e-mail newsletter

Title / rank

Name

Address

City / county

Postcode / zip   state / country

e-mail

I am interested in:

❑ Ancient world   ❑ American Civil War
❑ Medieval world   ❑ World War 1
❑ 16th century   ❑ World War 2
❑ 17th century   ❑ Modern warfare
❑ 18th century   ❑ Military aviation
❑ Napoleonic   ❑ Naval warfare
❑ 19th century

Please send to:

USA & Canada:
Osprey Direct USA, c/o MBI Publishing, P.O. Box 1,
729 Prospect Avenue, Osceola, WI 54020

UK, Europe and rest of world:
Osprey Direct UK, P.O. Box 140, Wellingborough,
Northants, NN8 2FA, United Kingdom

OSPREY
PUBLISHING

www.ospreypublishing.com

call our telephone hotline
for a free information pack

USA & Canada: 1-800-826-6600
UK, Europe and rest of world call:
+44 (0) 1933 443 863

Young Guardsman
Figure taken from *Warrior 22:
Imperial Guardsman 1799–1815*
Published by Osprey
Illustrated by Christa Hook

Knight, c.1190
Figure taken from *Warrior 1: Norman Knight 950 – 1204 AD*
Published by Osprey
Illustrated by Christa Hook

POSTCARD